"Everyone is replaceable. We may not want to think about that, but we need to plan for the future. We also need to think about who will lead and run our organizations. WHO COMES NEXT? walks leaders and managers through the process. This book is great for high-level corporate managers and military commands."

—Lt. Colonel Kathleen Grasse | U.S. Air Force (ret)

"In WHO COMES NEXT?, Mary Kelly and Meredith Elliott Powell tackle one of the most important and most avoided challenges in lasting business success: effective, strategic, and wise succession planning. In clear, practical and, most of all, actionable terms, these talented authors guide leaders to an absolutely vital destination — the future of their organizations once they step down. The authors provide a simple yet perfectly designed GPS to move executives and their organizations from fear to freedom as they pass the baton to the next leadership team."

—Brian Biro | America's Breakthrough Coach, Professional Speaker & Best-Selling Author

"I see the consequences of failures to plan all the time as an attorney. Sometimes it is because people just don't know what to do. WHO COMES NEXT? is about the mindset of planning for your replacement, as well as showing you the steps to take to be successful."

—Cris Carter | CEO, Cris Carter Law

"Succession planning goes way beyond the person at the head of the company. Depth on the bench is essential to ensure an organization's resiliency and contingency planning."

—Eric Holloway | U.S. Navy (ret)

"When businesses don't plan for leadership succession, it costs them money, momentum, and morale. WHO COMES NEXT? is the solution.

—Sam Richter | Founder/CEO, SBR Worldwide; Award-Winning Speaker & Best-Selling Author

"Top organizations are planning for their future success by making sure leaders have viable replacements who will fill positions with diversity of thought and innovative talent. Get WHO COMES NEXT? to make the process easy."

—Kelly McDonald | Author, *How to Work With and Lead People Not Like You: Practical Solutions for Today's Diverse Workplace*

"I think succession planning in small businesses is vastly overlooked. This book helps create a sense of urgency with both small and large organizations."

—John Stringfellow | Agent, Farmers Insurance

"This book is a comprehensive look at succession planning, but with a refreshing spin that favors the practical over the theoretical. It's applicable to any industry, and readers will benefit from action items, tools, and resources with every chapter. Succession planning has never been more critical, and this book is a must-read for any professional looking to answer the question, "WHO COMES NEXT?"

—Michael Delucchi | President and Chief Elevation Officer, The Elevate Group

"My clients need fabulous leadership speakers, and Meridith and Mary are amazing! Their material and program on succession planning fills a huge need as Baby Boomers retire and the next level of leadership takes over."

—Debbie Taylor | Founder, Taylor Made Events & Speakers

"Leaders today, especially sales leaders, need to make sure they are developing talent at every level. This guide shows you how."

—Don Cooper | President, The Sales Heretic

"Strong leadership and governance means learning from past and current leaders while planning for the future. Succession planning is a must."

—Ann Terry | Executive Director, Special District Association of Colorado

WHO COMES NEXT?

Leadership
Succession Planning
Made Easy

MARY C. KELLY, PH.D., Commander, U.S. Navy (ret)
AND MERIDITH ELLIOTT POWELL, M.B.A.

Published and Distributed by
SOUND WISDOM
PO Box 310
Shippensburg, PA 17257-0310
717-530-2122
info@soundwisdom.com
www.soundwisdom.com

Content Development and Editing: Susan Priddy (www.SusanPriddy.com)
Cover Design and Interior Layout: Kendra Cagle (www.5LakesDesign.com)
Virtual Assistant: Jennifer Lawrence (www.JenLawrenceAdmin.com)

ISBN 13 TP: 978-1-64095-388-8
ISBN 13 eBook: 978-1-64095-389-5

For Worldwide Distribution, Printed in the U.S.A.
3 4 5 6 / 25 24 23

DEDICATION

This book is dedicated to all the leaders who have had the
vision to build a business, the dedication to relentlessly pursue
its success, and the courage to ensure its future by turning it
over to the next generation of leaders.

TABLE OF CONTENTS

ACKNOWLEDGEMENTS

We'd like to send out a heartfelt "thank you"...

To all the friends, family, and team members who inspired us as we brought this book to life.

To those who introduced the two of us and encouraged us to work together.

To our partners (Susan, Kendra, Christine, and Jennifer), without whom this book would never be possible.

To Randy and Rob, for their endless support and willingness to put up with two, highly driven, always passionate, overachieving leadership experts.

FOREWORD
By Ed Hart

Whether you are working in a Fortune 500 company or a closely held firm, succession planning is not an *optional* conversation. It's mandatory. I know that from personal experience.

Over the past decade, I have consulted with dozens of family-owned businesses, and I've even worked in a few of them. The transition from one generation to the next rarely comes easy. Emotions, egos, conflicting opinions, and lack of clarity often complicate the process of selecting a new leader and making the change.

When I saw the title of Kelly and Powell's book, I was eager to dive in and read it. I fully understand why this information is so critical, and I was interested to see if they really had a formula to make succession planning easy.

They do!

Who Comes Next? is a great, step-by-step guide to help companies prepare for the future of their leadership from all angles. The authors provide their expertise on everything from the technical aspects of selection and transition to the emotional impact on outgoing leaders. They share their advice and wisdom on communicating throughout the process to get the rest of the leadership team or the other family members on board with the decisions made. They even give you all the tools you need to start creating a plan right away.

I applaud the authors for underscoring the urgency of this task. When family-business owners ask me about the best timing to establish a succession plan, I have a standard answer: "Yesterday. And if not yesterday, then today." It doesn't matter if the current owner is young and healthy or just stepped into the top role. Life is wildly unpredictable, and this process can't wait.

I strongly encourage you to use this book as a catalyst for action if you are part of the leadership team responsible for guiding your business into the future. Whether you are a current CEO, potential CEO, owner, heir, or anyone who supports those top roles, you can give your organization the stability to face whatever lies ahead by following the steps recommended by these authors.

Who Comes Next? should be required reading for every leader, as well as those of us who serve and counsel them.

Ed Hart is the President of the Hart Leadership Center and Host of The Hart Podcast. You can connect with Ed at www.HartLeadership.com.

INTRODUCTION

"What comes next?"

Pose that question to a team of top leaders, and prepare yourself for a veritable tsunami of strategic projections, detailed forecasts, multi-year plans, and a lofty set of corporate goals. Then try changing the question.

"Who comes next?"

Chances are, you'll experience awkward silence and some uncomfortable shifting in the chairs. This question regularly falls through the cracks for even the most intelligent, experienced, well-prepared professionals. That's a huge problem.

Leadership succession planning is the strategic process of answering that question: *Who comes next to lead our company when the current leaders are gone?* The goal is to solve the "people problem" faced by organizations of every size and shape: corporate entities, family businesses, closely held firms, nonprofits, and startups.

Great companies can't function without great leaders. That's always been a true statement, but now it comes with an ominous sense of urgency that we've never seen before. In our country today, the fierce competition for powerful leaders is accelerating at an unprecedented rate as the pool of available talent is shrinking.

Consequently, succession planning should no longer be a luxury; it's a put-down-the-status-report-and-get-started-on-this-right-now event. You get the idea.

THE PURPOSE

Every business must accept the reality that people are going to change jobs, move, retire, become ill, or even die. We can't control when or how key players are going to leave our companies, but we can minimize that impact by having an effective plan to replace them.

A common misconception about succession plans is that they simply identify the next CEO and maybe a few VP spots. The scope is actually much bigger and broader. An ongoing process rather than a one-time task, succession planning involves finding the right people, hiring them, training them, rewarding them, keeping them, and preparing them for pivotal leadership roles.

When developed and implemented properly, these plans can create a rich and continuous pipeline of top-level talent that will ensure the long-term sustainability and growth of our organizations. Granted, building and maintaining that pipeline requires some effort, but the results are well worth it. Companies that pursue succession planning gain an advantage by both developing home-grown leaders with the exact expertise and capabilities they need in the years ahead, as well as constantly searching for outside talent to augment the team.

THE REWARDS

Today, executive teams from the most successful organizations understand the intrinsic value of succession planning and use it to their full advantage. They diligently plant the seeds needed to grow exceptional talent, and they reap the rewards.

Specific benefits of proactive succession planning include:

- Ensuring the longevity of the organization through sustainable, strategic business planning.
- Creating a proactive strategy to attract and retain top talent.
- Clarifying the roles and responsibilities of leadership positions.
- Establishing a comprehensive system to develop employees and ensure their readiness for advancement.
- Providing smooth transitions when people retire or change jobs.
- Decreasing uncertainty and stress for shareholders, board members, leadership teams, employees, and customers.

OUR STORY

Long before we teamed up as co-authors, we discovered our common passion for helping companies use succession planning as a competitive advantage. Our backgrounds are vastly different, but we found a unique synergy in combining our expertise with leadership staffing from corporate America and the U.S. Navy. That is how this book was born.

Between the two of us, we have a wealth of experience working with organizations to weave the fabric of leadership continuity into daily operations. We know firsthand the kinds of concerns and struggles leaders experience, and we provide succession planning solutions that allow them to produce positive, long-term results. We are excited about the opportunity to share this dynamic, proven process with you.

Mary C. Kelly

- Leadership & Succession Expert
- Commander, U.S. Navy (retired)
- Military Logistics Professional
- Ph.D. Economist
- Certified Speaking Professional
- Corporate Advisor & Executive Coach
- Professor (*U.S. Naval Academy, U.S. Air Force Academy, Hawaii Pacific University*)
- Best-Selling Author of 13 Books

Meridith Elliott Powell

- Business Growth, Sales & Succession Expert
- Acclaimed Keynote Speaker
- Master-Certified Business Strategist
- Named Top 15 Business Growth Experts to Watch (*Currency Fair*)
- Executive Coach
- Online Course Instructor
- Former Sales Leader
- Award-Winning Author of 7 Books

See page 169 for complete author profiles.

THE PROCESS

In the chapters ahead, we guide you through a step-by-step process with a comprehensive blueprint to develop a meaningful succession plan for your organization.

At the end of every chapter, we include a diverse set of **Actions**, **Tools**, and **Resources** to further support your succession planning efforts. You'll find a summary list of the aids that pertain to the topics discussed, with a comprehensive collection at the end of the book.

 ACTIONS

Action plan checklists of specific steps required to develop, implement, and manage your succession plan.

 TOOLS

Assessments, evaluations, and handouts to support the process of establishing your succession plan.

 RESOURCES

Websites, videos, books, and articles to increase your knowledge and insights about succession planning.

You'll occasionally see the **Tools symbol** ✖ following a word or phrase. That's our way of letting you know we offer a specific tool to support that particular step in the process. You can find the exact page number of that tool by referring to the summary list at the end of the chapter.

We also want to personally invite you to visit our website for this book at **WhoComesNext.com.** We've packed this site with valuable resources, including **free succession articles**, **book bonuses**, **videos**, a **webinar**, an **online course**, and much more. We are constantly updating this site with new content, so check back often!

THE MAIN POINT

If you've ever felt overwhelmed or intimidated by leadership succession planning, this book is written for you.

It's a unique collection of information in a cut-to-the-chase-and-tell-me-how-to-do-it format. *Who Comes Next?* is a practical, straightforward guide to help you understand succession planning and...***get it done.***

When you reach the last page, you'll not only know what your succession plan needs to look like, but you'll also be well on your way to completing it.

Ditch the struggle.

This is leadership succession planning made easy.

Let's get started!

CHAPTER ONE

UNDERSTANDING
the Urgent Need for
Succession Plans

Thanks to global competition and the digital evolution, the pace of business today continues to escalate. Fewer employees scramble to cover the same intense workload. Higher demands and lower budgets often add fuel to the fire.

How are teams supposed to perform effectively under those conditions, day after day? In many cases, leaders rely on strategic prioritization. They focus on putting out the biggest fires first, and they hope the breakroom is fully stocked with coffee and Red Bull.

Continuously operating in crisis mode can make organizations dangerously shortsighted. When leaders are trying frantically to meet monumental daily challenges to survive, succession planning routinely drops to the bottom of the to-do list. On the surface, that seems understandable. Handling today's crisis feels mandatory; worrying about the future seems optional.

Nothing could be further from the truth.

Here's a prime example. When participants at a large conference in Baltimore attended a keynote by Dr. Bob Nelson about critical trends that would soon impact U.S. companies, they fully expected this professional "futurist" to talk about robotics and artificial intelligence. What they didn't expect from this man, who is also a professor at the University of Maryland, was an urgent conversation about the impending war on talent.

Yes, *the war on talent.*

In great detail, the futurist described a "perfect storm" of events within our society that are foreshadowing a full-blown crisis when it comes to staffing American businesses, particularly in leadership roles.

To give you some context for this perfect storm, let's look at the factors in play.

EXPLORING DEMOGRAPHIC SHIFTS

According to Gallup, approximately one-third of our country's total workforce in 2019 comes from the 75 million **Baby Boomers** (those born roughly 1944-1964). However, approximately 10,000 Boomers turn 65 years of age every single day. People within this huge population bubble are eyeing their 401(k)s and their calendars to determine when they can comfortably head for the exit and start their retirement.

Once those aging Boomers create a rolling mass exodus in the workforce, it seems logical to think that experienced professionals from **Generation X** (those born 1965-1980) could step in and fill the void. Unfortunately, the size of this group is much smaller. In addition, Generation X took a harder hit during the recession of 2008. Some members of this group suffered from extended unemployment during that time and never returned to the professional workplace, further draining the talent pool.

So what about the **Millennials** (those born 1980-1994)? This segment is larger than Generation X, but these younger professionals may not yet have the skills and experience to replace executive level Boomers who had careers that spanned decades. While some high potentials from this group might qualify for a speed pass into leadership positions, that solution has its drawbacks.

Research clearly shows that Millennials are wired differently than people in the older generations. For one thing, they are true "digital natives" and speak fluent technology. That creates a huge shift in how they approach challenges in the workplace and in life. Considering the sharp rise in online business transactions, this differentiation could be a strong advantage. With that said, the Millennials may also lack some of the interpersonal and communication skills that were essential before we relied so heavily on email and text messages.

Second (and perhaps a bit more controversial), Millennials grew up in an era with a marked change in parenting styles. According to sociologists, heavy parental involvement ("helicopter parenting") and consistent, hands-on direction became more prevalent during this time. Research now indicates that, generally speaking, this parenting approach may have reduced the Millennials' ability to think critically, solve problems, and handle adversity at the same level as their older counterparts.

In other words, substituting Millennials for Boomers or even Generation X isn't exactly an apples-to-apples switch.

All of these demographic shake-ups are creating the foundation for the predicted war on talent. Current leaders are ready to retire. Future leaders are less plentiful. Some surveys predict this disparity will create an estimated gap of ten million jobs with no one to fill them.

Imagine the ripple effect of those ten million empty desk chairs. Workplaces will see exhausted, grumpy employees trying to do the work of multiple people. There will be lost business opportunities. Human resources will be scarce to cover areas like R&D, quality control, or customer service. Without the necessary people to fuel the future of these organizations, they will fail.

Generations aren't the only thing changing the workplace, so we need to avoid blaming Millennials, Gen Z, or any other group for shifts we may not like. The expectations of employment have changed. Employees want to go to work, find meaning, bond with others while contributing to a higher purpose, enjoy what they do, and have the flexibility to work when and where they want.

Employers are adjusting to the changing needs of their people for a few reasons. First, the shifts make work better for everyone. Second, senior employees cite flexibility as an increasingly important benefit. Finally, if employers don't adjust, their top talent will move to an employer that will.

The futurist nailed it: The war on talent is coming. Or has it already arrived?

UNCOVERING TALENT SHORTAGES

In June 2018, the ManpowerGroup released the results of a sobering Talent Shortage Survey. Of the nearly 40,000 employers worldwide who responded, 45% said they are already struggling to remain completely staffed. In addition, the applicants they evaluated had fewer years of experience and demonstrated a lack of hard and soft skills.

Think about what that means. Less quantity *and* less quality. As employers try to fill critical leadership positions for the future, do they really want to be forced into taking anyone with a pulse? Adopting a beggars-can't-be-choosers position for staffing is certainly not optimal for companies that want to grow and thrive in increasingly competitive markets.

The urgency to address this problem is real. Vital leadership positions in companies like yours will eventually come open, and no one will be there to step in and take the reins.

Jonas Prising, ManpowerGroup Chairman & CEO, cut to the heart of the issue: "It's no longer a question of simply finding talent; we need to build it."

RESPONDING TO THE CRISIS

With the talent shortage looming, succession planning is the best solution for companies to ensure their continued success (and, in some cases, their existence). We're talking about the need for a strategic, focused, and ongoing plan that is appropriate for facing a confirmed crisis. A static list of names stashed away somewhere in a filing cabinet won't help.

When informed about the imminent staffing crisis, most companies agree that succession planning should have a higher priority. The problem is translating those intentions into reality. In some organizations, succession planning may be perceived as a touchy subject, so executives choose not to touch it. Other times, they fully intend to tackle it, but never get around to it.

A CNBC survey found that 28 million small businesses currently operate in the U.S., and more than half of the owners are over age 50. While 78% of those owners intend to sell their businesses when they retire, only 30% had taken the time to develop a viable succession plan.

For many organizations, the procrastination occurs because they have no idea how to get started. Admittedly, succession planning can be a complex process, and sometimes leaders feel overwhelmed by the unknowns and the obstacles. Will the soon-to-be-outgoing CEO be offended if they bring up the subject? Will employees start to feel anxious about the future? Will customers get nervous about the implications for them? All of those are valid questions, and we discuss the answers in the next three chapters.

Despite the fear of the unknown, avoidance and procrastination are no longer an option when it comes to succession planning. Organizations simply cannot afford to be shortsighted about this issue if they expect to survive during an extended battle for their most important asset — their people.

MAKING THE COMMITMENT

Given the urgency involved, we encourage leaders to take a realistic look at the need for succession in their own companies. If succession planning is not a priority for your executive team, it's time to move it to the top of the to-do list.

How do you stop making excuses and start taking action? Establish a succession planning team to work on this initiative, choosing representatives from your senior leaders and board of directors. This group would initially need to meet weekly, shifting to quarterly once the plan is in place. Before your first meeting, ask each team member to complete the **Obstacles Assessment ✂** as a reference for initial group discussions.

Make the commitment to protect your organization, your employees, and your customers with an indispensable strategy for future leadership.

 ACTIONS

☑ Make the commitment to start the succession planning process.

☑ Establish a team to lead the work on this initiative, choosing representatives from senior leadership and the board of directors.

☑ Ask your new team members to complete the **obstacles assessment** provided and use their responses to guide conversations in your early meetings.

☑ Communicate the urgency of this planning, based on demographic shifts and the impending talent shortage.

☑ Set up a schedule for regular team meetings to create positive momentum for the process (generally on a weekly basis, later shifting to monthly or quarterly).

 TOOLS

- **Obstacles Assessment: Planning Team** *(p. 126)*

 RESOURCES

- **WhoComesNext.com** (Online Course and Free Webinar)

CHAPTER TWO

EXPLORING
the Mindset of the
Outgoing Leader

Deciding to create a succession plan for your organization involves much more than simply jotting down a list of potential candidates to replace the person at the top of the org chart.

Think about this. For succession planning to be effective, it has to be championed from the top down. Owners, CEOs, and presidents have to be fully on board. They need to be able to speak about their eventual retirement with honesty and transparency, demonstrating their support.

So what happens if those top leaders flat-out don't want to discuss retirement or even think about a day when their names aren't on the corner office? What if you are...*ahem*...the person avoiding the topic? Either way, it's a serious roadblock. Uncovering how the senior leader really feels about stepping down might sound like a psychological detour, but it's a very important first step.

UNDERSTAND THE CHALLENGES

No one is more invested in the success of a company than its owner, president, or CEO. People who hold those titles worked hard to get there, and they often find their identity in those roles. They are emotionally all in. Needless to say, having a conversation about replacing them may stir up some deep feelings, even for the most confident, forward-thinking leaders.

From the perspective of senior executives, retirement may represent a sense of loss. Loss of purpose. Loss of power. Loss of structure, camaraderie and validation. They've spent their entire careers building a legacy, and that construction stops the day they have to walk away. We can't emphasize enough how difficult it is for great leaders to relinquish the companies they've been running for decades, especially if they built them from the ground up.

A perfect example is Frank Perdue, former CEO of the Perdue Chicken Company. You might recall his commercials and famous tagline: *"It takes a tough man to make a tender chicken."*

Frank's wife, Mitzi Perdue, wrote a book about the process of watching her husband step down after leading the company for 52 years.

"It was probably the hardest thing he had to do in his life — to try to walk away from work," Mitzi said. "He thought about that company every day until the day he died."

She explained that Frank dearly loved the business, and he poured his heart and soul into it. His identity as a person was essentially defined by the role he played in building the Perdue brand. One of the happiest days of his life was when his son Jim announced that he wanted to be part of the company.

Frank started preparing to turn the business over to Jim 10 years before his expected retirement. He trusted Jim implicitly. He was thrilled to know the company would remain within the family. But even into his seventies, he was reluctant to let go of his life's work. Stepping away felt like watching his identity and his importance dissolve.

After Jim took over the company, Frank would still show up at the office and want to participate. Mitzi shared that Jim would occasionally ask her to take Frank on a trip to help create a physical separation from work that might eventually lead to an emotional one. The transition was incredibly difficult.

OVERCOME THE RELUCTANCE

Like Frank, many senior leaders can't imagine life without their work, and it's important to be sensitive to that mindset.

If you are the person at the top, we encourage you to talk candidly with a trusted friend or advisor about your perceptions of retirement and the implications that would have for your daily life. Do you dream about it or dread it? Have you already made exciting plans for that phase of life? Or does it make you so uncomfortable that you vow to work every day until you can't physically keep going?

Some people admit to being all over that spectrum, but we frequently hear about the reluctance. Many of our clients have found it helpful to honestly articulate why they feel hesitant to step down and explore some ways to move past those feelings. Our **Obstacles Assessment** ✗ and **Five-Minute Leader Self-Assessment** ✗ may provide an avenue for those discussions.

We'd like to share some of the most common statements made by executives to push back against retirement, as well as our responses to help overcome the objections.

"I don't completely trust anyone to take over."

This is totally understandable. It may even be warranted. However, organizations can manage this sentiment by implementing policies that allow succession candidates to earn the leaders' trust and respect before the transitions.

- **Bring in more talent** with senior-level experience and proven track records.
- **Increase the responsibilities of in-house candidates** to help determine their readiness for executive leadership.
- **Provide more shadowing opportunities** directly with leaders so candidates can get an accurate view of more senior positions and their unique challenges.

"No one else knows what I know."

This is probably a true statement. Top executives do have a depth of specialized knowledge that made it possible for their companies to succeed, so sharing that information should begin immediately. These practices may help with managing the continuity of information within the leadership of your organization.

- **Ask the leader to create a knowledge management system** for the successor by starting now to map out day-to-day activities, challenges, and resources.
- **Set up open coaching sessions** where succession candidates can meet with top executives, ask questions, learn about strategic processes, and get a better understanding of what makes them tick.
- **Initiate a mentoring program** (if you don't already have one) and make sure your top executive is regularly pouring wisdom into those who are next in line. The most successful mentoring programs include two-way exchanges. Both senior and junior persons should learn from the time together.

"Other people won't be as dedicated to this job as I am."

Certainly, most C-level executives and business leaders are supremely dedicated to their work. It's their passion, their purpose, and their contribution to the world. With that said, other people also want the opportunity to contribute and demonstrate their commitment to the organization.

- **Learn to lead by asking questions,** which teaches employees to use their critical problem-solving skills and helps to build their confidence.
- **Create opportunities for feedback and input** (one on one, surveys, town halls), reminding employees at every level that their ideas matter and encouraging them to think bigger.

- **Allow employees to safely grow and learn from failures** as they expand their leadership knowledge.

"I'm the only person driving innovation."

If top leaders believe they are carrying that burden alone, they need to implement changes right away. Building a corporate culture that encourages and rewards creativity from every single employee produces breakthrough concepts, as well as higher levels of engagement.

- **Create idea exchanges** for employees to discuss their ideas about projects, products, or processes with leaders who will listen. When top executives know there is a system in place to actively solicit ideas, they don't feel the pressure to be the only ones responsible for creativity. Employees also feel valued when top leaders listen to and acknowledge their contributions.
- **Provide opportunities for employees to participate in optional projects,** such as serving on committees with a trade association or volunteering with a group to serve the community. These activities promote teamwork and creativity, while giving people the chance to learn, try out new skills, and engage with others outside of the workplace.
- **Institutionalize innovation** by ensuring you have a robust way to capture new ideas, new products, and new solutions. Be intentional about encouraging every single person in the organization to be creative with whatever they do, and listen carefully to their new ideas.

"The younger leaders don't want to work as hard as I do."

Your top executive has likely set a very high standard. They may be the first ones to arrive in the office every morning. They may be the last ones to leave at night. Young leaders may actually be intimidated by that relentless work ethic and wonder whether being in charge is even worth it. By providing a little more transparency about the job, you may be able to entice younger leaders to step up their game.

- **Ask senior leaders to make their calendars visible** so team members can see how they spend their days.
- **Give employees the chance to step into new roles** that expand their skills without the fear of being derailed or pigeonholed.
- **Ensure that top executives are delegating** frequently and effectively to reduce their workloads while giving others a chance to understand the complexity of senior-level decision-making and tasks.
- **Make the top job look like it is worth it,** and have open interviews about why top executives do what they do.

"What will I do if I don't go to work? I'll go crazy just sitting around."

Accomplished professionals who have the knowledge and skillsets to run an organization have plenty of options after retirement. In fact, we don't advocate sitting around the house. Research clearly shows that people need a purpose and a reason to get out of bed every morning. If they continue to apply their skills and talents in some way after retirement, they have a significantly lower risk of chronic illness, disease, and even death.

One helpful strategy is for executives to think about retirement as a process rather than an event. If they can begin to ramp up their involvement in other activities before they clean out their desks, they'll avoid that awkward gap of moving from a jam-packed calendar to one that's disturbingly empty.

If you sense that your top executives are worried about too much free time after retirement, ask them to complete our **Five-Minute Bucket List Plan.** ✕ Because they have been so focused on building their careers and their companies, many of their personal dreams have been ignored. Now is the time to revisit life goals. We can help to launch that process with these suggestions for activities that could add meaning and enjoyment to their post-corporate lives.

1. Get involved with a charity.

Charitable organizations always need smart people who can help them operate more efficiently, raise awareness, or increase donations. Former business leaders are typically a great match to help tackle those challenges. If they are passionate about a certain charity, they can easily find a way to share their skills and make a difference.

As an option, leaders could choose to start their own foundations in support of a particular cause. Bill and Melinda Gates took that route and now run the largest private foundation in the world.

2. Serve on a board.

Countless organizations could benefit from the advice and wisdom of a retired business executive. Serving on a board of directors is an excellent opportunity to add valuable leadership insights without the full-time commitment.

3. Be a mentor.

Retired executives who have a strong track record and time on their hands can "pay it forward" by mentoring others in the business world who are following in their footsteps. This is a satisfying way to share the 20/20-hindsight-view of strategic leadership and provide encouragement for young entrepreneurs, emerging management professionals, and future CEOs.

4. Enjoy a hobby.

Leaders may already have a favorite hobby — golf, tennis, gardening — and retirement will give them a chance to do more of that. In other cases, they may want or need to find something new that sparks their interest and creativity. They could take a course in photography or painting, join a fitness class, or learn a different language. These leaders simply need to think about what they've always wanted to do and make it happen.

5. Travel and explore.

Many senior executives end up stockpiling their vacation days. Before retirement, these leaders could benefit by taking real vacations and giving the next-in-command a trial run at being in charge. That strategy has remarkable benefits for current and future leaders alike.

Even if CEOs or presidents have loads of stamps in their passports, they may have only seen the airports and corporate conference rooms in those destinations. Retirement provides the opportunity to truly experience different cities across the globe — the culture, the food, the people. With the advantage of time and money, retired leaders deserve to dust off the bucket list of places they've always wanted to see (really see!) and start booking the trips. Make the plans. Buy the tickets.

6. Spend more time with family and friends.

Top leaders have often devoted countless nights and weekends to the company, and sometimes personal relationships get shortchanged. Retirement can help to restore that balance with precious time to reconnect with the important people in their lives. That could mean going on a family cruise, meeting a friend at the gym several mornings per week, or taking the grandkids to the park once a month.

REAP THE BENEFITS

Executive teams and boards of directors that take the initiative to understand the unique mindsets of their senior leaders with respect to retirement will have a much smoother transition for the succession planning process.

As leaders have honest conversations about their futures and express their concerns, they can begin to reframe the retirement transition as a new beginning rather than an ending. Once they recognize succession planning as a positive, essential step for the organization and for themselves, they can lead the entire company through the development and implementation in a smooth, seamless way.

We've had the privilege of watching many business owners and presidents make the mental shift that allows them to embrace the succession planning process. Instead of expressing reluctance or avoiding the topic, they are able to put a whole new spin on retirement and the value of structured succession:

- *"I built a great company, and I've got smart people in place to keep it thriving for decades to come."*
- *"My job doesn't have to define who I am."*
- *"I worked really hard for so many years, and now I get to spend time with my family. I deserve that."*
- *"I can be happy even when I'm not the CEO."*
- *"My contributions to the company will still be appreciated even when I step down."*
- *"I'm excited to get more involved with my community and make an impact in a different way."*
- *"This business is my legacy. I want to give it the best possible chance for long-term success, so I'm going to lead the transition instead of fighting it."*

☑ ACTIONS

☑ Acknowledge the emotional challenges involved when your senior leader confronts the idea of stepping down.

☑ Ask your outgoing leader to complete the **self-assessments** provided to help identify any limiting beliefs and **obstacles** that could be creating emotional roadblocks.

☑ Work with the outgoing leader to determine viable solutions for the obstacles uncovered.

☑ Support your outgoing executive in crafting a new vision for retirement using the **Five-Minute Bucket List Plan.**

☑ Encourage your top leader to embrace the benefits of succession and champion the process for the organization.

✖ TOOLS

- **Obstacles Assessment: Top Executives** *(p. 127)*
- **Five-Minute Leader Self-Assessment** *(p. 128)*
- **Five-Minute Bucket List Plan** *(p. 129)*

💡 RESOURCES

- *How to Make Your Family Business Last* by Mitzi Perdue
- *The Leadership Mindset: How Today's Successful Business Leaders Think* by Joe Calloway
- *In Case of Emergency, Break Glass!* by Mary Kelly
  WhoComesNext.com (Online Course and Free Webinar)

CHAPTER THREE

ANALYZING the Employee Impact

For those who believe succession planning only matters to the CEO (and the CEO in waiting), this chapter is important. Every single employee within a company feels the impact of changes in leadership. They want to know what's happening, and they have questions.

- *"Will the new CEO take the company in a different direction and eliminate our division?"*
- *"If the owner retires or leaves, will the company shut its doors?"*
- *"Will I still have a job?"*
- *"If my boss moves to another department, who will I report to?"*
- *"How will that affect my annual review and my bonus?"*
- *"Are there any legitimate opportunities for advancement here?"*
- *"How long am I going to be stuck in this position?"*
- *"What's the probability of getting a promotion at this company?"*
- *"What will it take for me to be promoted?"*

Employees care deeply about succession planning.

In a perfect world, a comprehensive succession plan would cover all jobs within an organization, providing a roadmap to the future with professional development plans for every employee. You can definitely get started on a smaller scale, but that's the ultimate goal.

From the employee perspective, broad-scale succession planning produces tangible benefits. Workers experience greater job satisfaction when they can see a path forward within an organization. Their confidence and self-esteem increase when they realize they are being coached, mentored, and prepared for a higher position. When employees are selected for new opportunities, they report greater levels of trust in the management team. Plus, loyalty increases dramatically when workers know the company is committed to supporting their professional development and helping them reach their career goals.

To capture those benefits through the process of succession planning, organizations need to make these actions a top priority:

BE TRANSPARENT

We discussed succession planning with one of our coaching clients, George, the CEO of a large firm. When we asked him if he had identified a successor, he told us he thought a woman at the company named Carrie would be a great candidate. She was a leadership superstar and had been with the organization for 12 years. Carrie was smart, poised, accomplished, and highly respected by her team.

We agreed that Carrie sounded like an excellent choice. The problem?

George had shared that information with us in confidence and didn't want anyone to know about his plans. He was concerned that Carrie might not work as hard if she knew that the top position would someday be hers.

As you might guess, that choice backfired. When Carrie was offered a CEO position with another company, she took it. She didn't know where she stood with George and assumed her career would be stagnant if she stayed there.

Lack of communication completely undermined George's plans to hand over the leadership torch to someone he trusted.

As you plan for succession, be diligent about keeping your employees informed. Transparency is a must. If you've decided to hire from outside rather than promote from within, be honest about that, too. Like Carrie, employees genuinely want to know where they stand in the bigger scheme of things within the organization. Keeping them informed will have a positive effect on attitudes and morale.

ALTER THE PERCEPTION OF TURNOVER

Humans tend to resist change. We love the familiarity of our normal routines, and we often feel uncomfortable when something smashes the status quo. It's just unsettling. That may explain why employees experience anxiety when it comes to the topic of succession planning.

One strategy to reduce that anxiety involves altering the perception of turnover among your teams. The U.S. military — known for its system of growing talent and promoting within the organization — provides us with great examples of **turnover by design.** ✖

When most people join the military, they come in at a low level and work their way up through the ranks. Most service members will only stay in the same jobs for two to three years. The expectations are clear. They need to learn quickly, take on increasing responsibilities and acquire the skills needed for the next level. The current job prepares them for the next position. Constant training, mentoring, and coaching are required.

This model surprises many civilians. How do you function with a 33-50% turnover rate in personnel every year? The expectation of constant change and transition is embedded in the whole process. People know change is coming. Instead of wondering if and when they will be moved to another position, they know in advance. They can focus on making the greatest possible impact in the time they're allotted at that post, while preparing to take on new responsibilities and ensuring that the people coming after them are set up for success.

What do these frequent moves look like?

Generally speaking, when people in the military switch to a new job, they leave turnover binders for those who are stepping into their positions. These binders (physical or digital) usually include copies of relevant policies, plans, and procedures; a personnel roster; and a list of resources with key people to contact. In addition, the binders include summaries of any ongoing problems, such as lawsuits, grievances, or investigations. From day one on the job, people in the military are thinking about what information needs to be transferred when they leave to establish continuity at that position. It's fluid and flexible and *all very normal.*

One person with significant expertise in this area is Eric C. Holloway, a retired captain in the U.S. Navy. During his 30-year career in the military, he was directly responsible for 2,000 highly trained personnel, physical assets of more than $40 billion, and the readiness and performance of nearly half of the nation's survivable nuclear arsenal. He was a commander of the U.S.S. Nevada (SSBN 733/Blue) and Submarine Squadron 20.

"Some say a commanding officer's legacy is the ship's performance six months after the change of command," Holloway explained. "On one hand, that underestimates the impact of the new commanding officer and the crew's ability to improve or atrophy quickly. However, that statement does highlight the Navy's deep commitment to succession planning.

"One of our main goals in any position is to make sure the person who follows us is highly successful. Outgoing commanders often start planning for change a year in advance, and incoming commanders at all levels are trained on the technical, non-technical, and leadership aspects of their jobs."

Holloway emphasized that departing leaders should complete a thorough assessment to identify strengths and weaknesses within themselves and their teams well in advance of a transition.

"The objective is not to achieve perfection before the change of command," he added. "The pursuit of such an unobtainable standard could demoralize the crew. Instead, knowing these weaknesses gives leaders insights into the relative degrees of risk that may require mitigation strategies, including training and qualification plans, focused supervision, and formal education. Incoming commanders can benefit from those insights and experiences, which elevates their potential for success.

"When outgoing commanders turn over detailed qualification plans with contingencies and backup strategies," Holloway concluded, "the new commanders are much more likely to reach their goals in a shorter time period. In addition, the strength of support from their predecessors leads directly to increases in daily performance, quality of life, and job satisfaction. The key to succession in the military is involving the entire organization rather than just selected individuals. It's a unique approach with a rich history of success."

Retired Navy Commander Theresa Kelly succinctly summarized this attitude. "Something my first Chief taught me was to lead so that, if you didn't show up one day, everything would run perfectly. When you make yourself irreplaceable, you are letting your organization down."

Companies in the civilian world could benefit by taking a page out of the military's succession playbook. We've provided you with a **Succession Turnover Checklist ✘** to get the ball rolling.

If corporate cultures were structured to help workers move regularly to new jobs — through promotions or cross-training opportunities — the employees would feel a greater sense of urgency and purpose. Professional development would become a pressing issue rather than something to do whenever the chaos dies down or the big project is finished. Employees would also feel more accountable to inform and educate the people who come behind them to fill their positions. Most importantly, they would approach change and turnover as an expected, even welcome, shift.

MAKE IT COLLABORATIVE

Employee input should be the heartbeat of a comprehensive succession plan. If organizations skip over the collaborative component of the process, they've completely missed the opportunity to make continuous improvements..

A company's human resources are its most valuable asset, so inviting them to provide feedback about a process that defines the future of those resources makes perfect sense. When you establish a channel for ongoing, open dialogue with your employees about potential leadership changes, you demonstrate a sincere respect for their opinions. Trust grows. Morale improves. Relationships flourish.

We recommend giving workers at every level an opportunity to take part in creating, developing, and improving a succession plan to increase your odds of success. Here's why: People who provide feedback on a project feel a greater sense of connection to the goal and a higher level of motivation to help it succeed.

We'll talk more in Chapter Six about the best way to collaborate with employees on this critical issue. Succession planning matters to employees, and their involvement is critical for organizational success.

☑ ACTIONS

☑ View the future of the company from your employees' perspectives — their wants, needs, attitudes, and motivations.

☑ Be transparent about all aspects of the succession process, keeping the employee point of view in mind.

☑ Explore ways to alter any negative perceptions of turnover, perhaps applying lessons from the **military's proven approach.**

☑ Use the **Succession Turnover Checklist** to help enable more seamless transitions.

☑ Create a channel for dialogue with employees to make succession planning a collaborative effort.

✖ TOOLS

- **Turnover by Design: A Military Approach** (p. 130)
- **Succession Turnover Checklist** (p. 131)

RESOURCES

- "The Time to Start Succession Planning is NOW!" By Mary Kelly (article available at ProductiveLeaders.com)
- "3 Strategies to Get Your Succession Plan Moving" by Meridith Elliott Powell (article available at MeridithElliottPowell.com)
- **WhoComesNext.com** (Online Course and Free Webinar)

CHAPTER FOUR

REVIEWING
the Customer
Perspective

We know many executives struggle to communicate with customers about their succession plans.

- *"Why would we bother them with that information?"*
- *"They don't need to know about our internal business!"*
- *"Why would they even care?"*

Short answer? Your clients, customers, suppliers, and retailers need to know that you are stable and planning for the future.

Take the case of Samantha, a 21-year-old college graduate starting her first professional job. She wanted to team up with a financial advisor who could help her make smart decisions early on in her career and begin investing in her future financial security.

She met with a wonderfully intelligent advisor named Greg, who was about 60 years old. He had great experience, and he patiently spent more than an hour educating her about personal finances. They had an excellent rapport, and she was ready to become one of his clients.

Samantha also felt the gravity of the situation, knowing she would be sending a percentage of every paycheck to this man for years to come. That prompted her to ask the bold yet awkward question: "I really like you, but what happens when you retire?"

Greg's answer was troubling, to say the least: "I *think* my son might take over the business someday."

While Samantha was briefly silent as she considered his response, the rapid-fire narrative in her brain was concerned.

- *"He might take over the business, but you're not sure?"*
- *"I've never met your son."*
- *"What are his qualifications?"*
- *"Does he share your investment philosophy?"*
- *"Is he a nice guy?"*
- *"And what if he doesn't take over?"*
- *"What happens to me and my account?"*
- *"Who do I contact if you get sick or when you die?"*

That level of uncertainty is disturbing, even for a 21-year-old novice investor. Greg wasn't prepared, and Samantha ultimately invested with a financial team who had a publicized succession plan.

Customers also experience anxiety during corporate transitions. For example, consider an electronics company that supplies parts to an automobile manufacturer. If the vendor suddenly gets a new management team, the car maker has legitimate concerns about the change. Will product quality slump as the new CEO starts slashing budgets? Will invoices have to be paid in 15 days rather than 30? Will we still be able to get enough products by our deadline to make our deliveries to dealerships?

People don't like uncertainty. When someone in a trusted role suddenly leaves, formerly loyal clients may leave as well. Trust is shaken when they are surprised and their plans are disrupted.

From the customer perspective, your succession plans have implications for them. They are important. Our **Customer Experience Assessment** ✖ may help you better incorporate that valuable point of view.

COMMUNICATE STRATEGICALLY

When you take responsibility for communicating with your customers about internal personnel changes, you are showing that you honor those relationships. The key here is to be proactive and keep the conversation at the appropriate level. No granular details. No drama or gossip. Just information about upcoming transitions that could have an impact on the business partnership. Customers (and potential customers) deserve that.

Samantha's decision not to work with Greg might have changed if he answered her question about his retirement in this way:

"That's a great question. Let me introduce you to the rest of the team. We have a solid plan in place that ensures continuity, so our office can serve you and your family for generations without interruption."

Effective and honest communication makes the difference between organizations that thrive and those that fail.

STRENGTHEN RELATIONSHIPS

People do business with people they trust. When you are open and honest with your customers about personnel changes, you are actively building that sense of trust. They will appreciate the information, and you can reassure them of the continuity surrounding their accounts. If the changes do have ramifications for their business, you're in the position to explain those and proactively make recommendations for adjustments.

You can also build trust by re-evaluating the way you structure your customer contact. If your organization is implementing a succession plan and expecting more fluid movement of your employees, you can lessen the impact on customers by switching from a single contact person to a team approach. That shift gives them confidence knowing their quality of service remains high when someone on the team gets promoted.

Leadership succession planning, at its core, is a change management process. Everything about your business (and your customers' businesses) is in a constant state of flux. As some people move into new positions, others will move on. Consumer preferences will shift. Technology will continue to evolve at lightning speed. In a few years, your organization will be providing products and services that haven't even been invented yet.

To stay relevant and valuable, we need to approach our employees and customers as partners. We need to share information, and they will be more likely to reciprocate. As their needs and requirements change over time, we are better positioned to keep the business flourishing because of the relationships we nurtured.

If you're exploring new opportunities to exceed customer expectations, we invite you to check out our **Five-Minute Customer Service Plan.** ✂

Believing that customers don't care about your succession plan is a dangerous assumption. Be strategic about keeping them informed, and you'll be rewarded with loyalty and longevity in your relationships.

 ACTIONS

☑ Evaluate the impact of potential leadership changes from the customers' perspective, using the **Customer Experience Assessment** as a starting point.

☑ Be prepared to communicate appropriate information about your succession plan with customers, reinforcing your commitment to them and addressing any potential objections.

☑ Use the **Five-Minute Customer Service Plan** to brainstorm ways to strengthen your customer relationships and minimize disruption during times of change within key leadership or contact positions.

 TOOLS

- **Customer Experience Assessment** *(p. 132)*
- **Five-Minute Customer Service Plan** *(p. 133)*

 RESOURCES

- *Be Amazing or Go Home: Seven Customer Service Habits that Create Confidence with Everyone* by Shep Hyken
- **WhoComesNext.com** (Online Course and Free Webinar)

CHAPTER FIVE

DEVELOPING
Your Plan's
Framework

As you begin to chart a course toward the future for your organization, you need to develop a comprehensive framework for the journey. Think of it as a succession roadmap. What's your destination? What route will you take to get there? And when do you need to arrive?

This chapter discusses clarifying your vision, selecting a succession model, and establishing a time frame for your progress. Once those elements are in place, we'll shift gears in Chapter Six to focus on developing a talent strategy that operates within this framework.

CLARIFY YOUR VISION

The toughest part about creating a working, viable succession plan is trying to figure out and prepare for leadership skill sets when we don't know what our organizations will provide or produce in 20 or 30 years.

Preparing for what we can't envision means developing a leadership team that can respond to change, think strategically, and harness the value of people and technology. How can we clarify a vision for the future with so many unknowns in the equation?

Consider the companies that produced eight-track tapes in the 1970s. Those corporate leaders may not have imagined that their industry could evolve to cassettes, CDs, DVDs, streaming, and digital downloads. The only thing that saved those organizations from extinction was the strength of their vision.

If their original vision was to produce affordable eight-track tapes, these companies didn't have a chance of surviving the radical industry transformation. But if their vision was to deliver music to customers in a high-quality, cost-effective manner, they would approach the industry in a very different way. By closely watching shifts in market demand, following a flexible path forward to meet their customers' fluctuating needs, and understanding the technology, the odds of success would have been exponentially better.

The moral of the story when it comes to your vision? **Think big, be proactive, and stay flexible.** Our Five-Minute Vision Plan ✕ can give you a jumpstart.

As you work to clarify your organization's vision, get input from your most important stakeholders, including members of your current executive team, emerging leaders, and the board of directors. Brainstorm individually and as groups.

The **questions** ✗ that follow may help to guide your discussions:

Think big.

- What are the big-picture benefits you deliver for your customers beyond your actual products/services (convenience, security, entertainment, comfort, etc.)?
- If your current products/services and delivery system become obsolete, how can you continue to provide the same benefits to your customers?
- How can you change the scope of your industry?
- What can you offer that would blow your competition out of the water?
- Do you have opportunities to meet other needs for your customers?
- Are there other target markets you can serve?
- How can you position your organization to be the recognized market leader?
- If you were going to start your company today, how would you do it differently?

Be proactive.

- What specific external factors have an impact on your business and industry — economic, financial, regulatory, technological, and competitive?
- What are the forecasts and projections for those external influences?

- How will those changes likely affect the products, services, and distribution methods you are currently using to serve your customers?
- What do you know about expected shifts in consumer preferences?
- How can you improve the way you build relationships with your customers in terms of communication, marketing, and sales?
- Can you provide solutions before your customers even realize they have a need?
- What steps can you take today to increase your efficiency, productivity, and performance in the years ahead?
- What can you do now to expand your revenue, profit, and shareholder value in the future?

Stay flexible.

- How can you make adaptability one of your organization's core values?
- How can you use agility and innovation as a competitive advantage in the future?
- How can you respond to the changing needs of your customers at a lower opportunity cost than your competitors?

Once you have gathered strategic input from your stakeholders, take a closer look at your company's existing vision statement. Does it need an update — or even an overhaul? Is it flexible enough to withstand the massive change that is undoubtedly ahead? Is it strong enough to provide your leaders with solid direction for generations to come?

When you take the time to refine your vision, you are establishing a foundation of continuity for your succession plan. It's your unchanging destination. Everyone in your organization will be working toward the same goal over time, no matter who is currently sitting in the corner office.

SELECT A SUCCESSION MODEL

The next step in the process is to determine the scope of your initial efforts in succession planning. Ideally, you'd have every leader fully on board to participate in the process and endless budget dollars to support the initiative. As you might guess, we have yet to meet anyone with those particular circumstances.

Realistically speaking, you can approach this process in a wide variety of ways. We recommend starting small and expanding over time. One of the worst mistakes in succession planning is to bite off more than you can chew at the beginning and then end up abandoning the whole project. It's a complex process with a multitude of components, so ease into it.

The best way to get started is by choosing a vision plan and framework that works for you, your team, and your organization. The model you select will define the tools and structures you'll use to implement your plan, identify specific needs, and target your development efforts. The model also adds language to your strategy and ensures that everyone understands the process for growing and rewarding talent within your company.

Here are three common **succession planning models** ✖ that are used by our clients, including the pros and cons for each approach. Sometimes organizations follow one of these models, as is. Others mix and match different elements. By selecting or building the most appropriate model for your company, you'll have a mechanism in place to consistently and continually develop your leadership bench.

Model #1: Open Recruitment

This model involves the most comprehensive process and is a long-term goal. To follow this, you determine the succession path for every leadership position at all levels of the company — C-suite to front-line personnel. Everyone in those designated positions is tasked with identifying their own successors, communicating with those individuals, and enrolling them in a formal training program provided by the company. With this type of broad initiative, accountability for succession is spread throughout the organization.

Advantages:
- Increases employee engagement and morale by involving most team members in the process.
- Ensures that candidates are well-trained and prepared.
- Provides a transparent path for talent to progress through the company.

Disadvantages:
- May seem overwhelming to attempt succession planning for every management and leadership position at once.
- Could be a drain on the organization because of the time and resource commitment involved.
- May lead to talent gaps, since candidates are not guaranteed to stay with the company.

Model #2: Specialized Recruitment

This model limits succession planning to a more specialized group within the company. Decision makers focus their planning on 3-5 positions that are vital to the success of the organization. In other words, without top-quality leaders in those key roles, the company would suffer in terms of cash flow, bottom-line results, and the customer experience.

An executive team identifies potential candidates to fill those positions once current leaders move on or retire. Before those departures, candidates receive targeted training and development in preparation for eventually taking on top assignments within the organization.

Advantages:
- Offers a faster, easier way to implement the succession planning process.
- Reduces the investment of time and money devoted to succession for the organization overall.

Disadvantages:
- Represents a single phase in the development of a comprehensive succession plan, which may require restructuring and expansion over time.
- Excludes mid-level management from the succession conversation and may discourage emerging talent.

Model #3: Outside Recruitment Model

If companies discover they don't have the talent necessary within their ranks to implement a succession plan, they may need to choose this model. Decision makers launch a thorough search for candidates outside the organization and, perhaps, outside of their industries. They may engage a qualified recruiting firm to assist with the complex process, or they may need a consultant to help assess candidates and provide necessary mentoring, coaching, and training.

Advantages:

- Provides an almost limitless talent pool.
- Enables access to new leaders with fresh ideas and different perspectives.

Disadvantages:

- Involves significant time and resources to find candidates with the appropriate skills, talents, and experience.
- Requires more in-depth training to get candidates up to speed on the company and the political landscape.
- May inject someone into the leadership team who has less loyalty to the long-term vision and could, ultimately, clash with the corporate culture.

As we mentioned before, organizations typically blend the strategies from several of these models to better suit their needs. For instance, you might get started with the Specialized Recruitment Model and make plans to move toward the Open Recruitment model in five years. After taking a closer look at your in-house talent, you might decide to tap succession candidates for four of your key positions and hire externally for the fifth one.

ESTABLISH A SCHEDULE

As mentioned in Chapter One, our biggest message about succession planning is to start now! However, we want to encourage you to pair that action-oriented attitude with the specificity of an actual deadline.

The schedule for succession planning may be naturally driven by an upcoming event. Perhaps your CEO expects to retire in three years. Two of your top VPs will be leaving in 12 months to lead subsidiary firms overseas. Maybe your company is being purchased by a larger organization in the next 18 months, and you have to prepare for the restructuring.

If you are designing your succession plan with an event like this in mind, use that timing as your deadline and work backwards in your calendar to schedule all the necessary tasks. We've provided a **scheduling tool ✗** to make that process easier.

At this stage in our discussions with clients, many of them breathe a sigh of relief and tell us they can manage this succession thing in 12-18 months. They've got this! Our response? Great! But... Establish a comfortable timeline for your succession planning, but don't lose track of the urgency.

You'll be surprised at how quickly the gap between "now" and "then" closes, particularly when the changeover for key positions involves attorneys and accountants. There's also a somber question looming in the background — one we'd all like to ignore. What happens if one or more of your top leaders are faced with a crisis situation tomorrow? A terminal medical diagnosis. A fatal accident. Devastating legal action.

Life is unpredictable. We can't change that, but we can be prepared with contingency plans.

Some of the most important people to involve in the succession planning process are your financial experts, insurance professionals, and accountants. These professionals provide valuable guidance with respect to the legal and financial implications of the plan you are considering. Building these relationships over time is critical during an HR crisis or a potential power struggle. You need to be able to reach out for help from trusted advisors who are already familiar with your organization's process and values.

When you use this type of methodical approach to build your succession plan, you're investing in the future of your organization. You'll be better prepared to maintain continuity of leadership despite the expected changes _and_ the ones you never see coming.

☑️ ACTIONS

- ☑️ Evaluate the trends and projections that impact the future of your company, your customers, and your industry as context for your planning (i.e., economic, financial, regulatory, technological, and competitive).
- ☑️ Use the **Five-Minute Vision Plan** and **Strategic Vision Planning Questions** to help facilitate your team discussions.
- ☑️ Brainstorm with your succession planning team to clarify your organization's vision, following the guidelines to think big, be proactive, and stay flexible.
- ☑️ Select or build a **Succession Planning Model** to help your company reach your vision.
- ☑️ Establish a preliminary schedule for creating and implementing the succession plan using our **Scheduling Tool**.
- ☑️ Begin to develop relationships with succession planning advisors, including attorneys and accountants who specialize in this field.

 TOOLS

- **Five-Minute Vision Plan** (p. 134)
- **Strategic Vision Planning Questions** (p. 136)
- **Succession Planning Models** (p. 138)
- **Succession Scheduling Tool** (p. 140)

 RESOURCES

- **WhoComesNext.com** (Online Course and Free Webinar)

CHAPTER SIX

CREATING
Your Talent
Strategy

Armed with your succession plan framework, you're ready to move forward and create a talent strategy. Sticking with our roadmap, these questions are answered next:

Who is interested in leading the organization? Who will stay with the company? Do we have the resources we need to get started? This phase of succession planning focuses on the people, but we still need to prepare some fundamental components to guide the process.

RETHINK YOUR CORPORATE STRUCTURE

In many cases, the succession planning process prompts you to think about your organization in a fresh way. Your refined vision may give you the perspective to see that future success would be greater if you restructure your leadership team or reorganize your lines of business. You might discover the need to add positions that don't currently exist. Some companies today are creating innovative roles, such as Chief Futurist Officer or Chief Freelance Relationships Officer. Use this opportunity to reimagine the optimal architecture for your human resources.

CHOOSE AN ORGANIZATION CHART

A dynamic organization chart becomes the graphic representation of the succession plan. We've provided a list of options in our Resource Guide, and you can find dozens more online. Select one that offers the level of detail to support your chosen planning model (targeting all management positions, the top five executives, or something in between).

DEVELOP CRITERIA

Instead of populating your new organization chart with names of potential candidates, focus first on descriptions of the talent required for future success. Skills. Experience. Values. Responsibilities. Basically, you are creating detailed **job descriptions** ✂ for all of the succession-targeted positions.

This exercise doesn't involve copying and pasting the job requirements you listed on LinkedIn the last time the position was open. The skills required for a particular job in the past will likely be quite different in the future, as our economy is increasingly driven by change. The leaders of tomorrow will deal with different customers, different competition, different markets, and different sales processes.

As you develop the criteria for each succession targeted position, pause to consider the changing skill sets required to compete in a totally different business landscape. Our **Five-Minute Skills Assessment** ✘ can help guide you through the process.

Few people would argue that the most important job description to define is the one at the very top of your organization chart: your incoming CEO or president. This person will lead the company into the future, so you'll want to spend extra time in creating the parameters for this position.

We have two suggestions to guide the process for defining the preferred characteristics of your incoming leader. First, identify the must-have **leadership competencies** ✘ for this position. Prioritize them and consider them non-negotiable. This is critical for every company, so establish an expectation for the highest professional standards. Some considerations might include:

- Business Judgment
- Conflict Management Skills
- Crisis-Management Experience
- Decision-Making Skills
- Emotional Intelligence
- Entrepreneurship
- Financial Acumen
- Industry Knowledge
- Influence
- Integrity and Moral Courage
- Interpersonal Skills
- Networking and Relationship Building
- Strategic Thinking
- Talent Development
- Vision

The second option is to work with a small, elite team to **create an "avatar" ✖** of the perfect future leader. In other words, identify the ideal attributes, characteristics, skills, and talents of the best possible person to assume control of the company when your current leader departs. This avatar gives you a more quantitative way to evaluate candidates as you compare them with the fictitious gold standard.

ANALYZE YOUR HR INVENTORY

Once your future-focused organization chart has been populated with the positions and job descriptions needed to keep your company on track, you'll be ready to determine how your current people can support those needs.

Here's the interesting thing about this part of the process. Creating the strategic organization chart with job descriptions before you assign actual people to those positions forces you to take your succession planning off auto-pilot.

For instance, Jake may have been with the company for 20 years, and everyone assumes he is next in line to become the VP of Operations. But is he really the right person for that job? Or is he the assumed frontrunner simply because of his tenure?

These are tough questions to answer. This process has the potential to upset some employees who assumed they would be promoted, but the long-term success of the company depends on moving the most qualified people into your targeted positions — not just those who have been waiting in line the longest.

So, what's the smartest way to solve this "people puzzle" and define the best career paths for your talent pool?

At first glance, this task might seem like a no-brainer. Antonio is a great accountant. Jill is a sales superstar. Nadia has brilliant social media strategies. But what if we don't know the whole story? Antonio is in leadership development training as part of his efforts to one day become the CFO. Jill is earning her MBA at night with hopes of landing the role of Marketing VP. Nadia aspires to shift into the IT department and become the top networking expert.

Do we always know what our people are doing? Do we know what they want? If we populate the organization chart based on our assumptions, we could be wrong. We need to know our people and what they want. That means getting them involved.

GET EMPLOYEE FEEDBACK

To create our talent strategy, we have to get the talent involved. We need to get their ideas so we can understand what they want and where they want to go within the organization in the years ahead.

If you're using the Open Recruitment Model, that means you'll want to engage in succession conversations with every leadership employee inside the company. That scope adjusts depending on the model you selected.

Leaders can gather vital feedback by asking their employees to participate in a **Five-Minute Career Plan** ✖ exercise and complete the **Leadership Development Plan Assessment.** ✖ Most importantly, they can engage in ongoing dialogues with employees, using the following types of questions.

- What part of your current job do you absolutely love?
- What part of your current job is your least favorite?
- What would you like to be doing more of?
- Are we challenging you enough?
- What role would you like to play within this organization long-term?
- What role do you view as a short-term goal??
- On a scale of 1 to 5, how ready are you to take on the next level of responsibility?
- What do you need to do personally to be ready to move up?
- What support do you need from the organization to help you become ready?
- If you were in charge, what would you change about the organization?

Through these conversations, leaders may uncover valuable information that directly impacts the succession plan, as well as pinpointing needs for training and development. Do some employees have skills that aren't being fully utilized? Are they less productive because they aren't working in an area that excites them? Do they eventually want to move into leadership positions? Or would they prefer to advance as subject matter experts? For succession plans to be effective, leaders need to factor in all of these employee preferences and subtle distinctions.

We can't emphasize this enough: Inviting employees to participate in succession planning creates a rewarding win/win situation. Besides helping workers gain clarity on their own career paths, this collaborative process makes them feel valued by the company. That leads to greater engagement, higher morale, and increased loyalty.

If your company wants to forge a stronger, deeper bond with its employees — your competitive advantage in the shape of talent — invite them to be active participants in creating your succession plan.

DESIGN TALENT PATHWAYS

At this phase in the process, you've gathered the feedback you need to begin developing a fluid version of your organization chart. Think about the expected career trajectory for each targeted employee, and then visualize how that flow of talent through the organization would impact results over time. In other words, begin designing talent pathways that will make sense for the organization and for the employees.

Some planning teams approach this task like it's a 1000-piece puzzle with only one solution. That is not true. Your succession plan should be a flexible model that is constantly subject to change. It's a journey with unavoidable detours, but multiple routes allow you to reach your destination.

Toss out the pressure to create something perfect and explore some options beyond your best-case scenario.

This exercise forms the basis for your **talent contingency plans**. The scenario planning technique that many companies use to develop good business strategies can also be applied to leadership succession.

In this context, you create a scenario to describe how the future might look if the core decision-makers on your organization chart flow through the process exactly as planned. Since the odds of that are fairly low, continue by developing some alternative scenarios that explore a range of possibilities and outcomes. For each scenario, analyze the possible effects on the company and identify any adjustments needed for your targeted training.

If you need a sanity check as you consider different talent options, you can always refer back to the map and ask some clarifying questions. Will this specific combination of talent help you achieve your vision? Will this improve or undermine your leadership bench strength? Will these potential moves support or frustrate your most valuable employees? How would your customers react to this particular cascade of changes?

Your goal is to uncover two critical pieces of information as you and your team move through this process. First, are there people currently in your organization who are not the right fit to take the company to the next level? This strategic approach to talent assignments can often make those less-than-optimal team members painfully obvious. These questions may also help you in your evaluation:

- Does this person have the skills and experience to make a significant contribution toward helping the organization achieve its vision?
- Does this person have the principles and values it takes to help lead our company?
- Are the preferences this person expressed for advancement realistic, given proper training?

Second, after you've projected career paths for all of your succession-targeted employees, identify what's missing. More specifically, what leadership skills are missing? What talent should you be recruiting from outside to give your company the best chance of success in the future?

The objective is to create a specific list of positions to be filled with external resources. This might include people at the executive level or entry-level employees who can keep the vision-focused talent pipeline full. This list of unmet, human resource needs will drive the next part of the process, which is the focus of Chapter Seven.

As we conclude our section on planning, we want to provide you with a quick recap of the ground you've covered and the important questions you've already answered:

Succession Plan Framework

Refined the vision	*What's our destination?*
Selected the model	*What route will we take?*
Established the schedule	*When do we need to arrive?*

Talent Strategy

Gathered employee feedback	*Who is interested in driving?*
Populated the organization chart	*Who will ultimately make the trip?*
Identified outside talent needs	*Do we have enough fuel?*

You've made incredible progress! Even better, you've got everything you need to begin implementing your succession plan.

☑ ACTIONS

☑ Reenvision the ideal architecture for your company's **human resources** as you move toward your vision and seek to maximize performance.

☑ Select an organization chart template to use as a graphic depiction of your new talent strategy.

☑ Populate the chart with job descriptions and criteria (rather than names of people) to define the exact **skills** and **leadership competencies** required for each targeted position.

☑ Get input from an elite team to create an **avatar** that represents the best possible person to assume control of the company when the current leader departs.

☑ Analyze your current HR inventory and start ongoing conversations with your succession-targeted employees about their aspirations using the **Five-Minute Career Plan** and the **Leadership Development Plan Assessment.**

☑ Integrate the information about your employees' strengths and preferences with the needs-based organization chart to determine optimal paths for talent to flow through the company over time.

☑ Create a detailed contingency plan to accommodate inevitable changes and any unforeseen circumstances.

☑ Identify any talent gaps in the succession pipeline and determine the human resources still required for future success.

⚒ TOOLS

- **Common Roles for Key Industries** *(p. 142)*
- **Five-Minute Skills Assessment** *(p. 144)*
- **Leadership Competency Assessment** *(p. 146)*
- **Leadership Avatar Exercise** *(p. 148)*
- **Five-Minute Career Plan for Employees** *(p. 150)*
- **Leadership Development Plan Assessment** *(p. 152)*

💡 RESOURCES

- Organization Chart Templates (available at WhoComesNext.com)
- **WhoComesNext.com** (Online Course and Free Webinar)

CHAPTER SEVEN

IMPLEMENTING
Your Succession Plan

With your framework and talent strategy in place, you're ready to officially launch your new succession plan. The implementation phase involves three distinct sections:

1. Filling in the gaps on your organization chart
2. Developing your talent to maximize their readiness for advancement
3. Creating a culture that inspires commitment and loyalty

RECRUIT AND HIRE

Attract top applicants.

Recruiting great talent for your succession plan starts long before you post a job description. Think about your company's brand awareness and image as an employer. Is your organization well known and well liked? Do current employees refer others to work here? Has your company suffered from bad press and negative comments on social media? Is your firm invisible? Do you have a great industry reputation?

When top professionals are deciding where they want to work, corporate reputation is a significant factor. Studies show that companies known for treating employees well get 10-20 times more job applications than their competitors. In the war for attracting talent, your reputation counts.

Upgrading your corporate image to attract top talent is a long-term project with broad scope. However, piece by piece, you can work to enhance the product you use to lure the industry's best performers. Are your offices attractive and comfortable? Is your location convenient? Are your compensation packages competitive? Do you offer any unique perks? How do current employees feel about working there? What do they say about the organization? Are they proud to be on your team?

In recent years, job seekers are increasingly asking another pertinent question — and it's sometimes a deal breaker. Does your company give back to the community? What kinds of corporate social responsibility do you practice? If your organization doesn't have a formal program to support a favorite cause or organize employees to participate in service projects, give that idea serious consideration. Besides attracting today's more philanthropically minded workers, greater corporate social responsibility also sends a positive message to customers and community members.

The key to increasing the quantity and quality of your job applicants is working to understand what current job seekers are looking for and do your best to meet those needs. If you can do that while consistently elevating your corporate image as a premier employer, you'll be able to keep your succession pipeline filled with exceptional talent.

Upgrade your online presence.

Your organization's website and social media accounts are scrutinized by potential employees. Be sure your online messaging is polished and targeted, providing an accurate representation of your corporate personality.

If ideal candidates are searching for jobs in your industry, can they easily find you online? Does your company stand out? Project the professionalism and attention to detail you want to attract in the people you're recruiting and, as needed, work to boost your SEO ranking to ensure you are visible to them.

Organizations that get online reviews should create a reliable system to monitor feedback in a timely manner. A one-star rating isn't a complete catastrophe, but responding quickly and appropriately is a necessity. Ignoring negative comments or responding inappropriately sends the signal that you don't care about customers. Express your sincere apology that their experience wasn't positive, and encourage an off-line discussion to resolve the problem.

Why does this matter for your succession plan? The way you handle your public image speaks volumes to job seekers who are trying to evaluate the culture and standards for your organization.

Use a strategic recruiting process.

When you recruit within the context of your succession plan, you're equipped to succeed with the support of an incredibly powerful tool: your detailed organization chart. You start the process with a complete profile of the ideal candidate for each position, including the exact list of skills and experience level required.

Not only can you use that information to craft highly targeted postings to advertise your open positions, but you also shift your recruiting from passive to active. Keep in mind that the most talented, successful professionals are probably already employed. They have jobs, and they may not see your posts about openings.

Instead of waiting for the perfect candidates to find you, proactively find talent by going to the places where you're most likely to connect with them. Our **Five-Minute Recruiting Plan** ✂ can help you reverse engineer the process.

To find great candidates, ask yourself some questions. If you were someone who matched the detailed profile for the perfect candidate, where would you be? What groups would you join? What events would you attend? What industry projects would you participate in?

The goals for you or your recruiting representative are to get involved with those groups and show up at those functions. Position yourself as a valuable contributor and be intentional about your networking. The relationships you build with superior talent through an active process could result in stunning additions to your organization chart.

Choose wisely.

Take the time to find the right people. It sounds obvious, but you might be surprised at how often hiring managers are pressured into rushing a recruitment decision. Interviewing and evaluating candidates can be very time consuming. Despite that, don't allow a "good enough" attitude to creep in when selecting pivotal leaders for your company. Keep your ideal characteristics in mind and maintain your standards. Getting this part right is crucial for the future success of your organization.

As you evaluate different candidates, push yourself to look beyond the resumés. Some people have impressive credentials, but they lack the soft skills that would make them great leaders. Be deliberate about assessing their intangible qualities. Do they have a strong strategic vision? Are they excellent communicators? Are they creative problem solvers? Can they build trust with a team? It's much easier to teach a strong leader about the intricacies of your company than it is to transform an industry expert into a highly influential leader.

Another angle to keep in mind during your hiring process is fairness. You'll want to be objective and remove any preconceived ideas or assumptions that could cloud your judgment during recruitment. For example, a study by Harvard University shows that 76% of people, both male and female, still perceive men as being more career oriented than women. Be aware of unconscious bias within even the best-intentioned hiring teams.

Other types of biases might include making judgments about candidates based on the way they dress or the schools they attended. Start from a "tabula rasa" so you don't inadvertently overlook someone with all the right skills and attributes to strategically complement your existing leaders.

Make a collective decision.

To avoid missteps, especially when hiring for top positions, get opinions and feedback about potential hires from other stakeholders besides the direct manager and HR representative. Plan to include other team members, some or all of the board of directors, and maybe even a corporate advisor before the process gets too far along. These people can provide outside perspectives and objective viewpoints that improve the quality of hiring decisions.

By positioning recruitment as a group activity, you also get the advantage of keeping the process more transparent. If you give the impression that hiring is a secretive project for anonymous committee members behind closed doors, you quickly end up with an atmosphere of mistrust, anger, and maybe even legal action. To avoid that, make the job criteria public, keep the process visible, and maintain open lines of communication throughout the company about hiring activities.

Create an optimal hiring and onboarding experience.

Here's a disturbing fact: According to the Wynhurst Group, 22% of new hires leave their companies within the first 45 days of employment. Ouch. If you've worked hard to find the perfect candidates to support your succession plan, don't let them slip away because of a rocky hiring or onboarding experience.

Take an objective look at your interviewing practices. Are they organized and efficient? Are interviewers respectful of the candidates' time? Is paperwork processed promptly? Are company representatives doing a good job of selling the company to potential future leaders? Are negotiations handled in a fair, professional manner so that candidates are left with a positive impression, whether they accept the positions or not? If you discover room for improvement, adjust accordingly.

Next, carefully review your onboarding process with fresh eyes. According to Randy Pennington, entrepreneur and president of Pennington Performance Group, "Organizations can't confuse New Employee Orientation with successful onboarding. If they assume people only need to learn how to sign up for benefits or use the computer system, they aren't setting people up for success.

"A solid onboarding process should accomplish three things for these new hires," he explained. "First, they need to feel a sense of confirmation about their choice to work at the company and believe their new co-workers sincerely want to support them. Next, they need to understand how their jobs contribute to meeting the organization's goals. Finally, they need to gain clarity about the company's values and see that the culture has high expectations for results, accountability, and attention to detail."

Does your onboarding process accomplish those objectives? Reevaluate the information imparted during this initial training time to ensure that it is relevant, targeted, concise, and easy to understand. As a way to measure those qualities, you might interview some employees who recently went through the onboarding process. Find out what they liked, what they didn't like, what they still don't understand, and how they think it could have been better. Use that knowledge to help you upgrade your onboarding practices.

This honeymoon phase of the new business relationship is critical to reinforce the decision to join the organization. Current leaders need to make onboarding a top priority and participate in creating a positive experience for new hires. We're tempted to repeat that last sentence five times in bold, but that might seem like overkill. Suffice it to say, this is a really big deal.

When executives take a hands-on approach to welcoming and orienting future leaders in those early days of employment, they are building the foundation for lasting business relationships. These connections will pave the way for smooth, succession plan transitions, while helping to eliminate any hints of buyer's remorse on the part of the new employees.

DEVELOP AND TRAIN

Grow your own talent.

While training and development are important for every organization, these endeavors take on even greater meaning through the lens of succession planning. When you apply a more strategic approach to learning, you can ensure that leaders in critical positions are fully prepared for their next stops on the organization chart. In a nutshell, we encourage you to take responsibility for growing your own talent and deepening your leadership bench strength.

Your organization may currently have some corporate superstars in the upper echelons of the employment roster. What do your second and third stringers look like at the moment? Do they have the skills and experience to become the next generation of top leaders for your company? That's one of the focal points for your succession plan.

Investing in leadership training and development is the equivalent of purchasing a smart insurance policy. Sports teams have back-up players. Broadway plays have understudies. Your organization needs to be packed with people who can step in, when needed, and continue to guide the organization toward its goals. If that's not the case, use this as an opportunity to build your talent bench.

Foster a proactive learning environment.

The most successful companies approach growth and learning as a large-scale, continuous process. Constant learning and professional development are mandatory in our quickly evolving environment.

The skills needed to perform a certain job today may be quite different than they were ten years ago. Required competencies will continue to evolve with changes in technology and the business landscape. For a succession plan to be timeless, the learning opportunities you provide for your employees should be just as fluid as your organization chart.

How can you create that type of learning environment?

Start by taking a more granular look at the talent pathways that emerged on your succession plan organization chart. Identify the training, tools, and coaching each person will need to be prepared for advancement to the next level. That list becomes the ground floor of your succession plan-era development program, allowing you to pinpoint the learning requirements for promotion. It's a rifle approach rather than a shotgun.

Next, evaluate your company's current training programs. Some organizations already have a comprehensive series of programs. Others outsource training to vendors or offer self-paced classes. Wherever your organization happens to fall on that continuum, take a serious look at the depth and the quality of your offerings. Find out what's working and what's not. What adds value? One of the biggest frustrations of top talent is wasting time on unhelpful, mandatory training.

With the benefit of knowing what you have and what you need, you're prepared to answer a pivotal question: What's missing? You have a defined way to fill in the gaps. While there are a myriad of training options available, you can zoom in on the perfect supplements to round out your own training curriculum. Do the research and add the education tools to give your future leaders exactly what they need.

This exercise may also help you to uncover some developmental dead wood, such as tired training courses with outdated information. Programs that could be shorter and, frankly, less boring. Just because you've always offered a certain training course doesn't mean it should be a permanent fixture. If it's unnecessary or uninspired, let it go. Prune back and find alternatives that create more impact to move your leaders forward.

Beyond the actual training classes you offer, look for opportunities to fold in experiential learning in the preparation of your future leaders. One of the best ways to assess candidates' suitability for the next level is to give them stretch assignments and watch them in action. This might involve asking them to step up and manage a team or champion a high visibility project — something that nudges them out of their comfort zones and gives them a chance to start flexing their leadership muscles.

Cross-training and rotating groups may also add value to your learning environment. Using this technique, you can provide new leaders and high potentials with a chance to work briefly in different functional areas of the company. That allows them to gain a broader view of the overall organization and better understand business processes from different perspectives.

Another powerful way to encourage the growth of top talent is to create 30-60-90 lists, which puts employees in charge of their own training. (Yes, really!) With this plan, leaders define what employees in new positions are required to know in the first 30 days, the first 60 days, and the first 90 days. Employees are expected to take ownership of the learning process by studying various resources, asking others to share information, and creatively acquiring the knowledge before the deadlines. This approach gives them a sense of purpose that often leads to greater engagement and success. It also allows employees to learn in the methods that work best for them, whether that might be research, shadowing, or hands-on projects. Check out our **30-60-90 Onboarding Guide ✄** for more specific details.

In addition, we suggest implementing a formal coaching and mentoring program to ensure that key succession candidates are receiving one-on-one guidance from leaders at the next level or above. This creates a built-in system for ensuring knowledge sharing and transfer, particularly as people advance through the company.

When organizations make obvious investments in learning, with money and with time, they send a loud message about being fully committed to the growth and advancement of their employees. Team members will quickly sense that continuous learning is part of the fabric of the organization, and they'll often adopt that same attitude. Check out our **Leadership Improvement Plan ✄** for a targeted approach to build a strong learning culture.

The bottom line? Nothing can propel a company toward future success like employees who are constantly hungry to learn more and have access to a buffet of development options.

Create customized development plans.

A recent Gallup poll showed that 81% of younger workers say they will leave an organization within two years if they don't have personal leadership development opportunities. They want the tools and opportunities to advance their careers. Scratch that; they *demand it*. If they can't see a clear path forward with your company, they'll be out the door. Pronto.

Thanks to your succession planning, you've already gathered some feedback from employees about their career aspirations as you designed your talent strategy. Continue the conversation. Managers should regularly touch base with employees to detect any changes in their expectations for career trajectories.

Sometimes this process shifts into what's known as *job crafting*—redefining certain positions to capitalize on the things some employees do really well. If you have people who can add value with unique skills, consider relaxing the organization chart a bit and creating some non-traditional jobs. Don't be afraid to use some innovative thinking and experiential learning to help you fully leverage the talents of your future leaders.

By integrating employee input with your laser-focused list of training requirements, course offerings and on-the-job experiences, you can now create customized development plans for each of your future leaders. You know where they want to go, and you have a variety of tools to help them get there. That's the perfect set of circumstances for mutually beneficial relationships.

Through personalized leadership development plans, you are providing your employees with concrete tools for them to visualize their future and, perhaps more importantly, to visualize their future *with your organization*. Your interest and investment in their careers show that you care about them both personally and professionally, creating an incentive for them to stay with you.

The results? Your succession pipeline remains full of talented professionals who have been trained and developed specifically for the leadership positions at your company.

ENGAGE AND RETAIN

Create a culture that supports your succession plan.

One of the most important ways to keep your employees on track is by giving them a work environment that keeps them fully engaged.

What does a great corporate culture look like? We'll try to paint the perfect picture for you.

Highly engaged employees ✘ thrive in a climate of teamwork and collaboration. They fully support the people ahead of them on the organization chart, and they mentor the people behind them. They believe in the company's big-picture vision. They understand how their individual contributions add value in reaching the larger goals, and they take responsibility for doing their part.

Morale is high. Turnover is low. Best of all, this maximized engagement culture is supported from the top down. The CEO and the executive team make decisions every day to reinforce an environment that values and supports the company's human resources. The natural outcomes of this culture are phenomenal performance and a steady stream of outstanding leaders.

Cue the orchestra and release the butterflies.

Yes, we're really passionate about employee engagement. That's because your succession plan depends on it. Your best leaders need to genuinely care about your company, and you need them to stay. Your culture can make that happen.

Admittedly, our idealized description of workplace engagement might be more of a lofty vision right now. That is why a vision where employees love coming to work matters. There is something magical about corporate cultures that transform employee mindsets and create wild loyalty. If you can tap into the power of an engagement-infusing environment, we guarantee you'll reap the leadership benefits for years to come.

Implement an ongoing communication campaign.

Communication is an integral part of creating a culture that supports your succession plan. Just to be clear, we're not referring to quick messages about job changes and leadership transitions. ("Diego got promoted. Lisa is taking over.") We're talking about a full communication campaign that helps employees understand how you plan for, find, hire, and develop your people. This includes letting people know what you're doing, why you're doing it, and how they are affected.

You might be surprised to discover that employees crave this kind of information. They expect real facts and complete information, not just fluffy junk mail that clutters the inbox and wastes their time. Your plan communications have to be clear, concise, consistent, and timely. When there's a communication void, rumors prevail and employees lose faith and confidence in their leadership and organization. This breeds uncertainty, which is unproductive.

The other essential aspect of your communication plan involves the two-way flow of information. Keep asking your employees for input and feedback. How do they feel about the leadership transitions in progress? Have they possibly misinterpreted any of your messages? Do they have suggestions or concerns? When employees are positioned as active participants, they will feel much more engaged in the succession process. Ask, listen, learn, and adjust.

Ensure ownership at every level.

If you want your employees to feel more engaged and accountable for their performance, help them understand their roles. They need to know how to be successful, including the incentives for reaching goals and the repercussions for falling short. Great leaders track results and progress, and they consistently follow through with rewards or consequences as needed.

Employees need to be in control of their careers and apprised of their progression opportunities. They have to take responsibility, but leaders have to help by setting expectations, providing feedback, and being consistent.

Another way to increase accountability is by encouraging your employees to think like business owners. Owners feel a professional connection to the outcomes of their performance, and they have a strong incentive to participate at the highest level. Every decision they make is in the best interests of their organizations and their customers. They are proactive. They don't waste time or resources. They take success personally.

Whenever employees are struggling to find direction, ask them this question: What would you do if you were the business owner? Over time, they will learn to use those thought processes as their decision-making benchmark.

Once you've inspired accountability among your employees and given them all the right tools, get out of the way and let them lead. Recognize that developing leadership skills takes time, and they will need a little space to figure some things out on their own. Demonstrate your trust and know that their sense of accountability will guide them through the process. Those developmental experiences will be extraordinarily valuable as they move up the chain of command.

Recognize and reward excellent behavior.

As of this writing, only 34% of employees describe themselves as engaged within the workplace, so leaders have their work cut out for them. Providing targeted incentives is often the fastest way to connect the dots between making an effort and generating real results.

If your employees are taking actions to support your succession plan, you want to actively reinforce that behavior. For instance, are they demonstrating peak performance every month? Are they embracing the learning environment and taking the initiative to enhance their skills? Are they doing a great job coaching and mentoring those who are at a level below them? Are they proactive about knowledge sharing and training their replacements?

These activities are direct evidence of employee engagement and should be rewarded. The obvious response is linked to their compensation. A bonus. A raise. A promotion. However, cash is certainly not the only way to accomplish the goal.

People genuinely want to feel appreciated, at work and at home. Leaders need to take notice of the those who go the extra mile and thank them for their positive contributions. As we have coached and consulting with leaders over the years, we're amazed at how many employees still have handwritten notes, emails, or other momentos from past leaders thanking them for a job well done. The power of appreciation goes a long way toward helping employees feel valued and connected with the larger purpose of the organization.

Other alternatives might be to nominate employees for awards, grant extra vacations days, or provide greater job flexibility. Leaders need to know their people well enough to know which incentives are most meaningful for each person.

To keep your succession plan viable, you need highly engaged employees who are committed to stay with your organization for the long term. The best way to retain top talent? Provide the right culture, the right information, and the right incentives.

✅ ACTIONS

- ✅ **Recruit** and hire the appropriate talent to fill the gaps in your succession plan organization chart.
- ✅ Increase the effectiveness and value of your onboarding process using the **30-60-90 Onboarding Guide.**
- ✅ Provide customized development plans for all targeted leaders and employees, and accelerate their growth using the **Leadership Improvement Plan.**
- ✅ Maximize your talent with a learning environment that provides strategic development courses, cross-training, coaching, and on-the-job opportunities.
- ✅ Create a culture, championed by the CEO, that inspires **engagement** and accountability.
- ✅ Develop an ongoing communication campaign to provide employees with consistent messages about succession planning efforts and activities.
- ✅ Work to retain employees over time by using the appropriate incentives, rewards, and recognition.

TOOLS

- **Five-Minute Recruiting Plan** (*p. 151*)
- **30-60-90 Onboarding Guide** (*p. 154*)
- **Leadership Improvement Plan** (*p. 156*)
- **Five-Minute Employee Engagement Plan** (*p. 158*)

☀ RESOURCES

- *Why Leaders Fail and the Seven Prescriptions for Success* by Mary Kelly and Peter Stark
- *Own It: Redefining Responsibility* by Meridith Elliott Powell
- **WhoComesNext.com** (Online Course and Free Webinar)

CHAPTER EIGHT

MANAGING
the Process

Succession planning is an ongoing process — a continuously evolving activity designed to sustain your company's growth over time. It's not something you can knock out at an executive retreat and cross it off your list. That means careful management is a necessity if you want to reap the full benefits of your plan for years to come.

In this chapter, we discuss the long-term maintenance required to keep your succession plan strong and vibrant, as well as the unique needs for transition management as you experience shifts in your top leaders.

LONG-TERM MAINTENANCE

As we've consulted with a wide range of organizations during the maintenance phase of their succession plans, we've discovered some specific actions that can help to keep the process moving forward.

Deliver on your promises.

By creating and implementing your succession plan, you are making a bold statement to all of your employees about the importance of talent within your company. We can guarantee that everyone on the payroll will be watching to see whether your declaration was an empty corporate platitude or a rock-solid promise.

In other words, follow through is everything.

Set up a schedule to meet quarterly with your succession plan team to maintain **accountability** ✖ and evaluate your progress. Check to see that succession plan-related tasks are taken seriously and implemented consistently across the board.

Are your management professionals working with targeted employees to establish and implement customized development plans? Do they provide coaching and mentoring on a regular basis? All of those activities will keep succession top of mind and facilitate an open dialogue about advancement with your employees.

From your perspective, are you offering all of the tools and resources necessary to spur professional growth? Are people aware of training options available and the benefits of participating in them? If your leaders want to send the message that learning is one of your company's core values, they need to hold themselves and their employees accountable for ongoing education, training, and professional progress.

Are you keeping employees informed about your succession process, opportunities for advancement, and any leadership changes on the horizon? Your leaders should be monitoring employee reactions to succession news, identifying any broad-based concerns or misunderstandings that need to be addressed. You should also make sure that your leaders have the tools they need to help **manage that change.** ✘

Drive the evolution of the plan.

To keep your succession plan relevant, revisit the organization chart and related components on a regular basis to identify anything that requires an update. Employees come and go. Economies fluctuate. Industry requirements change. Your flexible talent strategy needs to keep pace. Be prepared to make **course corrections** ✘ as needed.

You'll want to periodically reevaluate the training and development options you provide as your plan evolves. Do they contain the most current information, or have they become outdated? How are your programs rated in participant surveys? Look for opportunities to better meet the needs of your employees and freshen up any tired curriculum.

If you initially started the succession planning process on a small scale to make it more manageable, you may want to consider expanding it to cover more leaders or employees throughout your organization. Getting feedback about your existing succession plan from current and future leaders may help you determine the proper scope of your potential expansion.

Monitor growth and progress.

Pay close attention to the way targeted employees respond to the succession plan process. Who is taking the initiative to use the tools and resources provided by the company to enhance their growth? You may be able to identify some emerging leaders who were previously blending in with their peers. Likewise, you may discover a few people tagged as high potentials who actually display low levels of enthusiasm for growth.

In either case, those observations will provide you with beneficial insights for the progression of talent through your organization chart, as well as your subsequent recruiting needs.

TRANSITION MANAGEMENT

One of the most important phases in your succession plan is the changing of the guard: when one of your top leaders leaves and another one takes over. Your ability to manage these transitions with poise and integrity plays a big role in how employees perceive succession as a fundamental part of your organization.

Here are some steps to follow when you are expecting a top-level transition.

1. Consult with your advisors.

The departure of a CEO or president often has financial implications for organizations, particularly those that are publicly held. Get counsel from experienced attorneys, bankers, insurance professionals, and accountants to fully understand the impact of this departure, and keep in mind the perspectives of shareholders, employees, and customers as you navigate the transition.

2. Plan for the exit.

The first consideration is timing. If you have control over scheduling a senior leader departure, try to avoid transitions in the middle of a corporate crisis or a complex business deal. High-level personnel changes have the potential to undermine the perception of stability among customers and industry analysts.

Generally speaking, C-suite transitions should span 6-9 months or even longer in complicated circumstances. That provides adequate time for training and shadowing, plus a period of leadership overlap that allows plenty of opportunities for deep-dive knowledge sharing. More broadly, the new leader will need some time to establish rapport and build trust with the executive team from this higher level of responsibility.

3. Be transparent about the transition.

Let employees know, in advance, the relevant details relating to the transition. They need to know what to expect, when things will happen, and how they will be affected. Remember to provide them with updates as the situation fluctuates. Being open about leadership changes demonstrates the organization's commitment to partnering with employees through the succession process.

Since most people resist change and tend to think of it in a negative light, you can use these communications to help minimize the fear of the unknown among your employees. You can also get a head start on shaping attitudes and opinions about the transition by putting a respectful yet positive slant on the new opportunities ahead. Whatever messages you distribute should be honest, fair, and appropriately complete.

This kind of transparency has the power to pave the way for smoother transitions. Even better, it eliminates the sharp drop in productivity that can occur when everyone in the office is gossiping about the secretive meetings and unknown personnel changes.

4. Address residual changes.

While it's tempting to be laser-focused on preparations for the new CEO or president, take a closer look at cascading transitions that may occur across the organization. A shift of leadership at the top often creates a domino effect of changes, as other employees move up to new positions. Some may follow the executive to another organization, and others may decide to pursue different opportunities.

Once you establish a specific transition date for your senior leader, revisit the training and development requirements for those who will be shifting jobs at the same time. You may need to accelerate the development activities to ensure these employees will be ready to tackle their new roles. You also need to reassure and reinforce the roles of employees who choose to stay.

5. Prepare for the unexpected.

Remember those contingency plans? Sometimes your leisurely 6-9 months of leadership transition time gets trampled by unexpected events, and you will need to make a change...today.

Events happen. The CEO gets ousted after a heated disagreement with the board of directors. The president has a stroke in the middle of the night. The chairman unexpectedly resigns after news reports surface of an inappropriate relationship with an employee. The CTO is recruited by a global powerhouse or a tantalizing start-up. All of these succession plan-smashing scenarios are in today's headlines, so they are very real possibilities.

Let's take a moment and explore what that might look like. The crisis occurs. Then what? Essentially, the process you apply to manage the transition is the same, but on fast forward. Consult with advisors. Communicate to provide facts and minimize any rumors. Help to shift the narrative from the chaos to a discussion about "who comes next" and what that means going forward.

In times of crisis, your succession plan becomes a welcome lighthouse in dense fog. Your organization chart and contingency plans provide you with multiple options for how to flow your talent upward and fill whatever gaps are left by the sudden departure. If you've been diligent about methodically training and developing your employees, they will be ready to step up to the next level on short notice.

Even if you don't have the luxury of time to make a slow and smooth transition, your succession plan gives you the tools you need to respond as quickly and efficiently as possible.

✅ ACTIONS

- ✅ Establish a long-term maintenance strategy to keep your succession plan strong despite changing variables.
- ✅ Continue meeting with your succession plan team at regular intervals to monitor progress and reinforce **accountability** for staying on track.
- ✅ Drive the evolution of your plan over time: reevaluating the wisdom of your projected talent pathways, freshening any outdated development programs, and potentially expanding the scope of your process.
- ✅ Plan for the timing of top-level transitions if possible and consult with your advisors as needed.
- ✅ Carefully manage the challenges associated with transitions of key leaders, ideally orchestrating an overlap that allows for training, shadowing, mentoring, and knowledge sharing.
- ✅ Keep employees informed about the relevant details related to leadership transitions, and make sure leaders are trained to guide their teams through the **change process**.
- ✅ Be prepared to follow your contingency plans and **course correct** in crisis situations that result in the need for more immediate changes.

TOOLS

- **Succession Accountability Tracker** *(p. 160)*
- **Change Management for Leaders** *(p. 162)*
- **Course Correction Plan** *(p. 164)*

 **RESOURCES**

- **WhoComesNext.com** (Online Course and Free Webinar)

CHAPTER NINE

SUSTAINING
Family-Owned and Closely Held Businesses

When succession planning is applied to family businesses and closely held firms, the level of complexity can increase dramatically. Emotions and sentiments are involved. Personalities are more tightly intertwined. Operating decisions often impact personal finances, not just the balance sheet.

Let's delve into this topic by exploring some very revealing facts:

- More than 75% of privately held businesses today are family owned and operated.
- Family businesses provide more than 60% of the jobs in America and 80% of new job creation.
- Less than 40% of family businesses have a clear succession plan in place.

- While most owners hope to pass down their businesses to family members, the average success rate is dismal:
  - 30% of family businesses transition to the second generation
  - 12% make it to the third generation
  - 3% continue through the fourth generation

That explains why we wanted to devote an entire chapter to the distinct challenges of family businesses, which also generally apply to closely held companies. The **obstacles for family-owned businesses** ✕ are unique.

According to John Stringfellow with Farmers Insurance in Boulder, CO, succession planning in family-owned and closely held businesses is frequently overlooked. "I try to create a sense of urgency with my clients who are small business owners," Stringfellow explained, "but many of them are too caught up in the daily grind to think or act on what they need to do."

While the rules for developing, implementing, and managing a succession plan for a family business are basically the same, the process of choosing a successor requires a whole different level of finesse. We'll focus on that angle in the sections that follow.

THE PROCESS

Before family business owners can fully tackle the task of succession planning, they need to make sure their companies have a solid structure for daily operations. Many times, owners take a more casual approach in working with relatives to avoid creating a rigid, overly corporate atmosphere. But once family businesses have moved beyond the kitchen table to become legitimate, profitable entities, structure is no longer an option—and it's essential to support all the processes associated with succession.

If you are the owner, establish or strengthen a formal governance system that indicates how family members will be involved in decision-making. Clearly define responsibilities and set reasonable goals and objectives. Work with experienced professionals to develop an estate plan that eliminates any questions about ownership for those who are involved in the business.

This type of structure will give you the foundation to fully explore succession and create a strategy that fuels your family business for generations to come.

Start early.

Family business owners — especially the ones who built their companies from the ground up — naturally resist thinking about someone else taking over their role. That's an uncomfortable topic, so it's easy for them to procrastinate on succession planning. We're here to tell you: *Don't do it.* Start early!

Richard J. Bryan would strongly agree.

Bryan's father was the CEO of a 100-year-old, family-owned car and truck dealership worth $120 million in the U.K. When an illness forced his father to resign unexpectedly, the absence of a succession plan created pure chaos.

Bryan, age 28, was faced with taking over the company as the fourth-generation leader. While that alone was a challenge, he also quickly discovered the business was losing $3.5 million per year. He openly admits he made plenty of mistakes and was not prepared to step into that role.

"I had neither the skills nor experience to run the business and lacked credibility with our bank and manufacturer partners," Bryan explained. "Worst of all, there was absolutely no plan of what to do when my father became ill. It was a very stressful time in my life."

Somewhere within that stressful time, Bryan realized he needed assistance. He reached out to a seasoned business specialist who helped him turn the company around and achieve profitable growth. A pivotal part of that process was creating a succession plan to keep the business going, even in difficult times and unexpected circumstances.

If you own or operate a family business and want to preserve its integrity long-term, give succession planning the time and attention it deserves.

Anticipate conflict.

The primary goal for succession planning in family businesses is exactly the same as it is in other corporate entities: identify someone who is qualified to take over the top leadership position. The difference? The candidates often include children, siblings, other relatives, or even a spouse. Understandably, making that choice can trigger some intense emotions.

Whatever decision the current CEO makes about a successor, there's a fair chance that Thanksgiving dinner will include turkey and resentment. That's just a fact of life for family businesses. Despite the potential for awkward moments, the owner has a responsibility to all of the family members and stakeholders to act in the best interests of the company. Admittedly, protecting the family legacy can involve making some tough calls.

Evaluate strengths and weaknesses.

Family business owners who begin considering candidates for succession need to honestly evaluate each person's strengths and weaknesses. The goal there is to uncover whether someone's unique skills are a good match for the ones required to lead the company.

This task can be difficult when it's clouded by the natural feelings associated with family members. How many parents think their children can do no wrong? Spoiler alert: Love, pride, and the unquestionable benefit of the doubt can seriously skew business decision making.

We recently heard about two brothers who owned and operated a medical testing lab that served regional hospitals and doctors' offices. Since they always dreamed of keeping the business in the family, they hired their niece to run the lab and manage the team. She was bright and personable, and it seemed like a perfect solution.

Six months later, they realized it was a mistake. Employees were disgruntled, and their niece was overwhelmed and frustrated. She simply didn't have the leadership and technical skills required to take the company into the future.

In what must have been a heart-breaking meeting, the brothers shared the news and told her she might be better suited for a different role in the company. Today, she runs the sales and customer service teams for the lab. She's absolutely passionate about her job, and she has grown that part of the business by more than 50%.

Finding the right match of skills for a future leader is a make-it-or-break-it exercise. Without the right match, the consequences can be very expensive.

What does that mean for family business owners? They have to be prepared to make candid assessments about the skills of their beloved relatives who are potential successors. If those skills don't match, the owners also have to be prepared to have some difficult but necessary conversations.

Identify the best successor.

As owners and CEOs narrow down the search for a successor, they need the discipline to temporarily remove the emotional component of this decision and objectively answer some key questions:

- Who is the most qualified person to take over as leader today? In five years? In ten years?
- Is this person interested in leading the company?
- Does this person aspire to be the leader for the right reasons?
- Does this person have the right match of skills and experience required?
- Does this person have the wisdom to handle business challenges and the complex family dynamics?

- Is this person genuinely committed to the success and long-term growth of the company?
- Would the business be better served by bringing in someone from the outside?

We worked with a man who had been CEO of a family business for 40 years, transforming the company value from $100 million to $2 billion. He had seven children and made the decision to put his oldest daughter in charge when he stepped down. That seemed like a fair and logical choice to him, although the rest of the family did not agree with the decision. Morale suffered.

After running the business for two years, his daughter was hospitalized with addiction issues. The former CEO hated having to replace her at a time when her self-confidence and ego were fragile, but he knew it was necessary. Unfortunately, his other children were not interested in helping since they were left out of the original succession decision. Things did not go well.

Ultimately, a non-family member was brought in to manage the daily operations of the business. All seven of the children still have ownership, but only three are actively engaged in the company.

The moral of that story?

Family business owners need to be more strategic about choosing their successors, and they need contingency plans. Picking someone to be the top leader shouldn't be based on birth order or tenure with the company. Instead, the best choice of successor should have the right qualifications to run a business and the right attitude to earn respect among the family members.

Consider the impact.

Before making a final decision about a successor candidate, owners should think about the reactions and responses that a particular choice might elicit from the rest of the family, other employees, and customers. How would people feel about this decision, internally and externally?

Credentials aside, this future leader will set the tone for the work environment and become the face of the organization in the marketplace. That deserves some consideration.

In the event an outsider may be chosen as the successor, owners need to carefully investigate the financial impact of that move. Inheritance issues will likely be affected. If the wealth of the family members is tied up in the business, transferring ownership to an outsider could put all of their financial futures at risk. Sometimes selecting an outsider is still the best decision, but that choice should be made within the full context of implications.

Methodically follow the process.

Once a successor has been identified for the top leadership position, the process should include the same steps.

- Develop a full succession plan that covers a broader set of family members in leadership positions.
- Create a culture that supports succession, tapping into the shared vision of family members to build a legacy that lasts for generations.
- Communicate regularly about succession with equal parts of confidence and compassion out of respect for coworkers who are family members.

- Make professional development a mandatory deliverable, with extra emphasis on preparations for the incoming CEO or president, specifically regarding formal training, exposure to all areas of the company, coaching, networking with major customers and vendors.

Move slowly during transitions.

The most successful transitions in closely held or family businesses occur over an extended period of time. Unless a crisis dictates an immediate shift, the slow and deliberate pace allows an overlap in leadership that helps everyone to adjust to the change.

We had an opportunity to work with a dentist named Jane. She used this approach to succession with outstanding results.

Jane owned a small dental practice in the northeastern U.S. for more than 30 years. She had eight employees. Several times over the years, she had tried to bring in a younger associate who could eventually buy the business, but she couldn't support another expensive salary without decreasing her revenue.

Jane was understandably concerned about succession. If she wanted to retire, she needed to sell the practice to someone who could perform on her level. This dentist would not only need the right skills and experience, but also be able to pay the price Jane wanted to charge for her practice and office equipment.

At age 52, Jane hired a succession consultant who helped her develop a 10-year plan that would allow her to retire at 62.

In the first three years, Jane focused on making her practice more marketable. She invested in quality talent, efficient business systems, and proven operating processes. She updated her strategic plan, developed employee manuals, held team meetings, and defined roles and responsibilities. She created new programs to attract patients and developed an onboarding process to streamline the operations. All of these changes significantly increased the value and potential price of her practice.

Jane and the consultant began actively searching for potential buyers in the fourth year. A strong candidate emerged after several years, and negotiations for the sale took more than 12 months. When the sale was final, Jane still had one year left before her target retirement date. She stayed on during that time to help her patients and the new owner make a smooth transition.

Once she retired, Jane enjoyed peace of mind that her practice, her employees, and her patients were in good hands. The best part? She made more money from the sale than she ever imagined, thanks to her patience and intentionality.

Closely held and family businesses are a vital part of our economy, but we know from the statistics that they frequently struggle to survive for multiple generations. The challenges they face are, of course, not all related to talent and leadership transitions. However, if more of them adopted the principles of strategic succession planning, we firmly believe their rate of long-term success would be significantly higher.

☑ ACTIONS

☑ Ensure that family-owned or closely held businesses have a formal governance system, established goals, and an estate plan that specifies the legalities of ownership.

☑ Be proactive and strategic about selecting a qualified candidate to eventually replace the top leader.

☑ Methodically develop and implement the complete succession plan: preparing a talent strategy, building a succession-supportive culture, advocating continuous learning, and communicating frequently.

☑ Carefully plan transitions and, when possible, move slowly to minimize disruptions.

✖ TOOLS

- **Obstacles Assessment for a Family Business** *(p. 165)*

RESOURCES

- *Handing Over the Reigns: A Concise Guide to Succession Planning* by Richard J. Bryan
- *The Successful Family Business: A Proactive Plan for Managing The Family and The Business* by Edward Hess
- *How to Make Your Family Business Last* by Mitzi Perdue
- **WhoComesNext.com** (Online Course and Free Webinar)

CHAPTER TEN

TROUBLESHOOTING

The heart of every succession plan is the talent — the people who truly make the company what it is. Even with a world-class plan in place, you may find that some of those people are occasionally uncooperative, anxious, or downright obstinate. Did anyone immediately come to mind? We understand. This is normal and expected.

In the pages ahead, we provide our professional advice and some compelling examples to help answer the following questions:

"What if our CEO won't discuss succession?"

"What if our CEO refuses to step down?"

"What if the heir apparent to our family business is the wrong person?"

"What if high turnover is undermining our succession plan?"

"What if our employees are overly anxious about succession?"

"What if some of our leaders just won't leave?"

"What if our CEO won't discuss succession?"

Top leaders often feel like their identities are defined by their titles, so the concept of retirement can be intimidating. You know the business risks of ignoring succession. The executive team or a trusted advisor will need to take the lead and start the conversation.

One technique is to change the way you approach the topic. Begin by reframing succession as a broader process that will support the long-term growth of the company. (In other words, it's not just a glorified replace-the-CEO project.) Stay focused on the sustainability of the business rather than on the circumstances of the individual departing. Point out that succession isn't always triggered by a retirement or a firing. The current CEO might be offered an exciting new position, or the company might expand in a totally different direction. Keep it positive, and the conversation will be much easier.

Within that context, you can point out the personal benefits of a gradual transition to your senior leaders, such as the support from other top executives, the opportunity to take on new responsibilities, or the freedom to take more time off. Helping CEOs look at the big picture of succession allows them to slowly move past the fear of an abrupt ending.

The next step is getting the CEO deeply involved in succession — inviting full participation and encouraging the top leader to champion the process. Ask for their input. Apply their feedback. Make sure they feel a sense of ownership and investment in the success of the plan. Understanding and involvement can go a long way toward getting a reluctant CEO on board.

We worked with an organization that was facing this same challenge. Terry, the CEO, was adamant about avoiding retirement discussions, even though he was starting to show signs of slowing down. We came in as advisors to help guide the process and met with him for multiple conversations about the value of succession planning. Although he was clear about not being ready to leave, he was eventually open to finding someone who could begin absorbing more of the daily operations.

We set up a task force within the company's board of directors and asked Terry to serve as chair. Over the next six months, this committee collectively defined the qualities of the perfect succession candidate and started a search. Terry was able to personally design his role in working with the incoming CEO, giving him control over the parameters of his evolving responsibilities. Once he visualized his purpose beyond the transition, he could mentally make space for another person to enter the picture.

The company soon found an ideal candidate, and the gradual leadership change was remarkably easy. Two years later, Terry was still serving on the board in an advisory role, while thoroughly enjoying his retirement. He was able to disengage on his own terms.

If your CEO shuts down every conversation about retirement, change your approach and be persistent about helping your organization find a path forward.

"What if our CEO refuses to step down?"

Sometimes the succession plan is in place, but the transition hits a roadblock. This happens frequently.

A brilliant inventor named John was in his seventies and still running the company he founded. When he had a health scare, he decided it was time to retire and let his 35-year-old daughter, Susan, take over the business. After the retirement party, Susan spent some time moving her things into John's former office.

Unfortunately, John failed at retirement within the first 24 hours.

He walked back through the door the next day as a self-appointed senior advisor. He wanted to attend meetings and weigh in on decisions. He even decided he wanted his office back.

Any way you look at it, John's presence was severely undermining Susan's authority. Many of the long-time employees had watched Susan grow up and still viewed her as a little girl. They continued looking to John for direction and approval. Susan also had plans to explore some fresh directions for the business, but her father was highly vocal about his opposition to anything new.

Susan was trapped in a holding pattern between the past and the future, with no idea how to proceed. She adored her father and respected the company he built. She recognized he was struggling to let go. But for the sake of the company and her own sanity, she needed to lovingly kick him out.

That's when she called us. Luckily for Susan, we had experience with this type of situation. Through a series of meetings, we were able to bring more structure to John's retirement and help him step away without losing his sense of purpose.

We guided Susan and John to more clearly define their roles and responsibilities in terms of daily operations and decision making. John needed some boundaries (an understatement!), and this process helped him understand why the future of the company depended on Susan establishing her leadership.

We also encouraged John to take a bigger role in the organization's philanthropic efforts, which was an idea he thoroughly relished. He was actually excited to devote more time to fundraising on behalf of the company for his favorite cause.

Within three months, the situation drastically improved. Susan had settled back into the corner office, and John was finding the beauty in a more hands-off approach. Did he enthusiastically offer his opinions whenever asked? Absolutely. But he was learning to watch from a distance while admiring his daughter's growing confidence and accomplishments.

If your CEO, president, or chairman refuses to step down, take the initiative to address the situation before it has a negative impact on your employees or your bottom line. Reach out to advisors who may be able to help broach the subject. You'll need some patience to change the top leader's perceptions about succession, but you'll be ahead of the game if you apply a proven strategy.

"What if the heir apparent to our family business is the wrong person?"

Hindsight is 20/20. Perhaps your family business has an obvious successor, and that person has expected for years to eventually step into the top leadership position.

Except now it's obvious that's a really bad idea.

Maybe the heir apparent is lazy or feels entitled. This person might not fully understand the business or even care about continuing the legacy. Health issues might be involved. Perhaps an ugly divorce shifts control of the company to an ex-family member. There are a wide range of reasons why the once perfect successor suddenly becomes a threat to the future of the organization.

The solution? **Contingency plan.**

Even if you firmly believe succession for your family business only has one path, push yourself to come up with an alternative. Take the time to consider what happens if your best-case scenario becomes the worst. Your company cannot survive without strategic leadership, so you may have to stretch the boundaries in search of an alternative CEO. Give consideration to another relative, a valued employee, a close friend, or an outsider. Find someone you trust and know will care about the business as much as you do.

Be prepared. Difficult conversations will be part of executing your back-up plan. You may be able to lessen the blow by working with a team of advisors who can present a business case for making the change. Do your best to stay focused on the impact on the company rather than making it personal. If possible, suggest some alternative roles or options for participation that will help to preserve the relationship with the former successor.

Most importantly, renew your conviction to do what's best for the company. Hopefully the heir apparent will one day understand the decision and, on some level, even be grateful for avoiding what could have been a catastrophic failure. That level of self-awareness takes time.

"What if high turnover is undermining our succession plan?"

Turnover is certainly disruptive when your goal is to cumulatively develop talent to progress through your organization. We've discovered that some companies can veer off track if they promote people based on the wrong criteria.

One of our succession clients named Amanda contacted us with concerns about an unusually high rate of employee turnover. She was diligently following the talent development strategy in her succession plan but, over and over again, excellent employees were leaving. On their own or with encouragement to do so. Amanda was frustrated and needed some advice.

After an analysis, we uncovered the problem. The company had gotten into a rut of promoting top performers — people who were doing an outstanding job in their current positions. Unfortunately, great performance in one particular job is not always an indicator of success at a higher level. The skill sets are different. Variables are constantly changing.

Amanda's company needed to adjust its filter for promotion to find future-ready employees — those who can anticipate change, handle adversity, inspire teams, generate action, and get results. Skills and talents certainly matter, but leadership ability (or potential) is much more closely linked with employees' long-term success, job satisfaction, and loyalty.

We helped Amanda to adjust her criteria for promotions using this strategy. We also encouraged her to be more specific in defining what she needed from her leaders and ensuring they were fully trained before advancing them to the next level. By making these changes to her process, Amanda was able to reduce turnover throughout the next 12 months while increasing employee engagement among her leadership team.

If you are noticing a higher than normal amount of attrition among your previous top performers, step back to determine whether leadership skills are a primary requirement for advancement in your organization.

"What if our employees are overly anxious about succession?"

Maybe you've seen the signs of uncommitted, apprehensive team members. You start to see an increase in tension and people calling in sick, along with a drop in productivity. A tense atmosphere that makes collaboration ineffective.

All of these symptoms could be the result of anxious employees who are worried about the changes associated with normal succession. They might be concerned that their jobs are in jeopardy or worried that new leaders might have expectations they can't meet. Those are natural responses, but the business impact can be detrimental. Nervousness, stress, and depression don't lead to a positive work environment or breakthrough results.

As leaders, it's our job to help people cope with the uncomfortable feelings that come with change. We've found that our clients get a better handle on this challenge when they understand a little about the psychology behind it.

When people are trying to process change, they often go through four distinct phases: denial, resistance, exploration, and commitment.

THE J-CURVE OF CHANGE

TRANSITION PHASES

4. Commitment to Problem Solving

"Growth requires change."

"We can make this work together."

1. Angry Denial

"My boss can't leave."

"I'm not reporting to someone else."

3. Cautious Exploration

"Are there are upsides?"

"Maybe this will work if…"

2. Active Resistance

"Why would they do that?"

"This will never work."

The big take-away? Things will get worse before they get better. Expect that. But know that they *will* get better if you manage change properly.

Sympathetically guide your employees through the first two phases, while working to shorten the time it takes them to reach exploration and commitment. Dealing with change is like a muscle that can be strengthened over time. If you're consistent about helping employees process the uncertainty of change, your team will get better and better at responding to the continuing shifts of your succession plan.

"What if some of our leaders just won't leave?"

The root of this problem is identical to that of outgoing CEOs. Walking away from a legendary career, even one that has run its course, equates with losing identity, importance, and income. Retirement may symbolize a lack of purpose and the threat of boredom.

Frankly, legal limitations may prevent you from removing current leaders who have outstayed their welcome, despite the need for new talent. You can, however, set the stage for a future in which employees view retirement as a welcome evolution in the flow of your succession plan.

Just like you use training and development to prepare your talent for advancement within the company, you can also implement programs that prepare senior leaders for retirement.

- Highlight company benefits related to retirement as part of your compensation package, including IRAs, 401(k)s, and SEPs.
- Provide financial education to ensure that employees understand their retirement options early and be proactive about helping them meet their goals.
- Communicate regularly with employees to emphasize the importance of securing their financial future.
- Let employees know that the company needs advance notice about retirement to put proper resources in place.
- Offer incentives to those who are able to take early retirement.
- Consult with an attorney and/or HR officer for clarity about what you should and shouldn't say when having retirement discussions with employees to prevent claims of age discrimination or harassment.

Employees who are financially and emotionally confident about retirement make more rational decisions about the timing of their departures. Your caring support garners trust and creates a positive atmosphere for departing leaders and the organization.

CONCLUSION

Succession planning is an essential and powerful process for businesses of every size and shape.

It enables organizations to fully leverage their leadership talent. It prepares teams to handle whatever the future holds. It produces a competitive advantage for companies to achieve sustained, long-term growth. Most importantly, it deserves to be elevated from a whenever-we-get-around-to-it task to an urgent priority.

Our primary message:
Don't wait. Start now.

Without a succession plan, the future of your company could be in jeopardy. To underscore this message, we want to share one last example.

The three leaders of a regional insurance company wanted to strengthen their edge by adding a fourth partner to the firm. Each one of them had strengths in their own areas: Operations, Finance, Sales and Marketing, and Mergers and Acquisitions. These partners, all healthy and in their 40s, had a brilliant synergy and ambitious plans for the future.

Stiff competition was disrupting the insurance industry at the time, so the leadership team was perpetually consumed with production and meeting steep goals for growth. Despite advice from several consultants to prepare a succession plan, the daily demands of business got in the way. "Not now," they said. Not enough time. Not necessary.

For two years, the partners got away with that strategy. Until they didn't.

One of the partners — an avid runner — shockingly died from a heart attack while preparing for a marathon. During the exact same week, an audit showed that another partner was embezzling money. He was fired immediately. This impressive leadership team with incredible momentum was slashed by 50% in a matter of a few days.

The two remaining partners were absolutely stunned. They had no expertise in the other two divisions, and they had no back-up plan to cover those areas. In the excruciating months that followed, the partners worked around the clock in an effort to keep the firm afloat. New problems emerged daily.

Clients wondered if the company would survive, and many of them took their business elsewhere. Employees worried about their job security and started sending out resumes. Internally and externally, the company suffered some heavy blows.

The irony of the situation was not lost on the two remaining partners. Although they worked in the insurance industry and dedicated their careers to helping people prepare for disasters, they failed to plan for their own.

The next two years were touch and go for the firm, but the partners managed to claw their way out of the crisis. They learned the hard way that succession planning isn't an option or a luxury or a someday project. It's about making the commitment now to protect the future of your company, no matter how busy you are.

Because, as these partners discovered, anything can happen tomorrow.

That statement is true for all of us. Whether we are just starting out in a business or inching closer to a target date for retirement, succession planning matters. For every person. For every organization.

We hope this book inspires you to take action and prepare for leadership succession within your own business. Wherever you are in the planning process — well under way or about to make the leap — we encourage you to take a close look at the sections that follow.

 The **Comprehensive Action Plan** is your complete, step-by-step guide for tackling all phases of the succession planning process.

 The **Tools Library** includes all of the assessments, evaluations, and handouts to support you in developing and sustaining your plan.

 The **Resource Guide** provides you with a full list of every resource mentioned in the book.

Additionally, we invite you to visit our website at **WhoComesNext .com** for extra materials to make the planning process even easier. That was our driving goal with this book. On the home page of our site, you'll find details about how to register for our online succession planning course and how to access our free webinar. Check back often, since we regularly add new materials!

Thank you for joining us on this journey of discovery to answer that all-important question that businesses can't afford to ignore:

Who Comes Next?

We wish you the very best of luck and a long, prosperous future.

COMPREHENSIVE
ACTION PLAN

Your Step-by-Step Guide to Succession Planning

Check each step when complete. Tools are available to support any action items listed in bold.

GET STARTED

- [ ] Make the commitment to start the succession planning process.

- [ ] Establish a team to lead the work on this initiative, choosing representatives from senior leadership and the board of directors.

- [ ] Ask your team members to complete the **obstacles assessment** provided, and use their responses to guide conversations in early meetings.

- [ ] Communicate the urgency of this planning, based on demographic shifts and the impending talent shortage.

- [ ] Set up a schedule for regular team meetings that will create positive momentum for the process (generally on a weekly basis, later shifting to monthly or quarterly).

UNDERSTAND THE DIFFERENT PERSPECTIVES

☐ Ensure that everyone involved in planning recognizes the diverse perspectives of people who are impacted by the succession process.

Senior Leaders

☐ Acknowledge the emotional challenges involved when your senior leader confronts the idea of stepping down.

☐ Ask your outgoing leader to complete the **self-assessments** provided to help identify any limiting beliefs and **obstacles** that could be creating mental roadblocks.

☐ Work with the outgoing leader to determine viable solutions for the obstacles uncovered.

☐ Support your outgoing executive in crafting a new vision for retirement using the **Five-Minute Bucket List Plan**.

☐ Encourage your top leader to embrace the benefits of succession and champion the process for the organization.

Employees

☐ View the future of the company from your employees' perspectives — their wants, needs, attitudes, and motivations.

☐ Be transparent about all aspects of the succession process, keeping the employee point of view in mind.

☐ Explore ways to alter any negative perceptions of turnover, perhaps applying lessons from the **military's proven approach.**

☐ Use the **Succession Turnover Checklist** to help enable more seamless transitions.

☐ Create a channel for dialogue with employees to make succession planning a collaborative effort.

Customers

☐ Evaluate the impact of potential leadership changes from the customers' perspective, using the **Customer Experience Assessment** as a starting point.

☐ Be prepared to communicate appropriate information about your succession plan with customers, reinforcing your commitment to them and addressing any potential objections.

☐ Use the **Five-Minute Customer Service Plan** to brainstorm ways to strengthen your customer relationships and minimize disruption during times of change within key leadership or contact positions.

DEVELOP THE PLAN

☐ Evaluate the trends and projections that impact the future of your company, your customers, and your industry as context for your planning (i.e., economic, financial, regulatory, technological, and competitive).

☐ Use the **Five-Minute Vision Plan** and the **Strategic Vision Planning Questions** to help facilitate your team discussions.

☐ Brainstorm with your succession planning team to clarify your organization's vision, following the guidelines to think big, be proactive, and stay flexible.

☐ Select or build a **succession planning model** to help your company reach your vision.

☐ Establish a preliminary **schedule** for creating and implementing the succession plan.

☐ Begin to develop relationships with succession planning advisors, including attorneys and accountants who specialize in this field.

☐ Reenvision the ideal architecture for your company's **human resources** as you move toward your vision and seek to maximize performance.

☐ Select an organization chart template to use as a graphic depiction of your new talent strategy.

☐ Populate the chart with job descriptions and criteria (rather than names of people) to define the exact **skills** and **leadership competencies** required for each targeted position.

☐ Get input from an elite team to create an **avatar** that represents the best possible person to assume control of the company when the current leader departs.

☐ Analyze your current HR inventory and start ongoing conversations with your succession-targeted employees about their aspirations using the **Five-Minute Career Plan** and the **Leadership Development Plan Assessment.**

☐ Integrate the information about your employees' strengths and preferences with the needs-based organization chart to determine optimal paths for talent to flow through the company over time.

☐ Create a detailed contingency plan to accommodate inevitable changes and any unforeseen circumstances.

☐ Identify any talent gaps in the succession pipeline and determine the human resources still required for future success.

☐ **Recruit** and hire the appropriate talent to fill the gaps in your succession plan organization chart.

☐ Increase the effectiveness and value of your onboarding process using the **30-60-90 Onboarding Guide.**

☐ Provide customized development plans for all targeted leaders and employees, and accelerate their growth using the **Leadership Improvement Plan.**

☐ Maximize your talent with a learning environment that provides strategic development courses, cross-training, coaching, and on-the-job opportunities.

☐ Create a culture, championed by the CEO, that inspires **engagement** and accountability.

☐ Develop an ongoing communication campaign to provide employees with consistent messages about succession planning efforts and activities.

☐ Work to retain employees over time by using the appropriate incentives, rewards, and recognition.

MAINTAIN THE PLAN

☐ Establish a long-term maintenance strategy to keep your succession plan strong despite changing variables.

☐ Continue meeting with your succession plan team at regular intervals to monitor progress and reinforce **accountability** for staying on track.

☐ Drive the evolution of your plan over time: reevaluating the wisdom of your projected talent pathways, freshening any outdated development programs, and potentially expanding the scope of your process.

☐ Plan for the timing of top-level transitions if possible, and consult with advisors as needed.

☐ Carefully manage the challenges associated with transitions of key leaders, ideally orchestrating an overlap that allows for training, shadowing, mentoring, and knowledge sharing.

☐ Keep employees informed about the relevant details related to leadership transitions, and make sure leaders are trained to guide their teams through the **change process.**

☐ Be prepared to follow your contingency plans and **course correct** in crisis situations that result in the need for more immediate changes.

TOOLS LIBRARY

FOR THE PLANNING TEAM

Obstacles Assessment

For each statement below, check the box that applies to you as a member of the succession planning team. You can use your responses to prompt productive conversations in your group meetings. Through those discussions, you'll begin to pinpoint the biggest challenges ahead in the succession planning process.

1. **I know exactly how to start the succession planning process.**
    ☐ Yes   ☐ No   ☐ Maybe

2. **I know the specific plans and timing for our current top executive to step down.**
    ☐ Yes   ☐ No   ☐ Maybe

3. **I feel confident discussing succession with the top executive and openly planning for an incoming leader.**
    ☐ Yes   ☐ No   ☐ Maybe

4. **I know how to objectively identify the skills and requirements needed for an incoming CEO/President to be successful in the future.**
    ☐ Yes   ☐ No   ☐ Maybe

5. **I know which leaders want to advance within the organization, and I understand their career goals.**
    ☐ Yes   ☐ No   ☐ Maybe

6. **I am confident that our senior leaders will remain with the company under a new CEO or President.**
    ☐ Yes   ☐ No   ☐ Maybe

7. **Our organization currently has a leader who could successfully move into the top executive role when needed.**
    ☐ Yes   ☐ No   ☐ Maybe

Obstacles Assessment

Each statement below represents a mental or emotional obstacle related to stepping down as a senior executive. Check the boxes that apply, and use your responses to guide a candid conversation about your concerns with the succession planning team.

1. **I am worried about not being replaceable.**
    ☐ Yes   ☐ No   ☐ Maybe

2. **I am worried about being easily replaced.**
    ☐ Yes   ☐ No   ☐ Maybe

3. **I am worried about a loss of identity.**
    ☐ Yes   ☐ No   ☐ Maybe

4. **I am worried about a loss of prestige or power.**
    ☐ Yes   ☐ No   ☐ Maybe

5. **I am worried about not having purpose and meaning in my life.**
    ☐ Yes   ☐ No   ☐ Maybe

6. **I am worried about being bored.**
    ☐ Yes   ☐ No   ☐ Maybe

7. **I am worried about the future success of the organization.**
    ☐ Yes   ☐ No   ☐ Maybe

8. **I don't completely trust anyone else to take over.**
    ☐ Yes   ☐ No   ☐ Maybe

9. **I don't think anyone else will be as dedicated to this job as I am.**
    ☐ Yes   ☐ No   ☐ Maybe

10. **I am worried that my replacement won't have the knowledge or experience to do the job.**
    ☐ Yes   ☐ No   ☐ Maybe

Five-Minute Leader Self-Assessment

Change can be difficult—especially if that change involves stepping away from a job that has defined your career. Being prepared has likely been a big part of your success, and you now have the opportunity to help your company prepare for the future. If you've been resisting the topic of succession, this self-assessment may help you get to the heart of the problem.

1. **What worries you about leaving or retiring?**

    _____

    _____

2. **What impact would stepping down have on these areas of your life?**

    Daily Schedule _____

    Friendships _____

    Family Relationships _____

    Social Activities _____

    Sense of Purpose _____

    Self-Esteem _____

3. **What emotional obstacles might be causing you to avoid discussing succession?**

    _____

    _____

4. **What worries you about having someone else take over your job?**

    _____

    _____

5. **What are the potential benefits of stepping down from this position?**

    _____

    _____

Five-Minute Bucket List Plan

Chances are, the chaotic pace of leadership didn't leave you much mental space to think about your bucket list. What are your dream activities? Pause now for five minutes, and let your creativity take over.

I'd like to learn how to _____

_____

I'd like to travel to _____

_____

I'd like to see _____

_____

I'd like to participate in _____

_____

I'd like to compete in _____

_____

I'd like to take a class about _____

_____

I'd like to spend more time with _____

_____

I'd like to pursue _____

_____

I'd like to own/build _____

_____

I'd like to volunteer for _____

_____

I'd like to give back by _____

_____

Turnover by Design
A Military Approach

People in the military know that they will change jobs and locations every 2-3 years. Even with that level of purposeful turnover, the military remains mission focused and combat ready. Could your organization benefit from following this proven approach? Answer these questions to get started.

1. **Reiterate the vision.**
   How do you clarify and reiterate your vision throughout the organization?

   _____

   _____

2. **Train constantly.**
   Have you created a learning environment for your employees? Are training and development viewed as innovative and important or mandatory and mundane?

   _____

   _____

3. **Plan for your replacement's success.**
   Do your employees take pride in supporting their replacements, actively helping them navigate the challenges of the new job?

   _____

   _____

4. **Share knowledge.**
   Do your employees create turnover binders and lists of resources to pass on to their replacements as a strategy to shorten the learning curve?

   _____

   _____

5. **Do you assign sponsors to help new people navigate their new environments?**

   _____

   _____

Succession Turnover Checklist

Employees can create more seamless transitions for their replacements if they prepare a "turnover binder" (physical or digital) as a guide. These binders should include answers to the following questions, along with any supporting documents.

Time:
- ☐ What do you spend most of your time doing?
- ☐ What meetings do you have daily?
- ☐ What meetings do you have weekly?
- ☐ What meetings do you have monthly?
- ☐ What meetings do you have yearly?
- ☐ What conferences do you or should you attend?
- ☐ When do you complete your strategic planning?

Goals:
- ☐ What are the current goals and objectives?
- ☐ How often are these reviewed?
- ☐ Who do you review them with?

People:
- ☐ What does the organization chart look like?
- ☐ Who is on your team?
- ☐ When are performance appraisals due?
- ☐ What personnel gaps do you have?
- ☐ Can you review your team's information with HR?
- ☐ How deep is your talent bench?

Budget:
- ☐ What does your budget look like?
- ☐ Did you meet your budget last year?
- ☐ When is the budget due?
- ☐ Where do you store copies of budgets from the last 5 years?

Legal:
- ☐ What regulations do you need to understand?
- ☐ Are there any pertinent legal situations?
- ☐ Are there any pending lawsuits?
- ☐ Are there any potential lawsuits?
- ☐ Who do you turn to for legal advice/guidance?

Customer Experience Assessment

To determine customer perspectives about your potential succession changes, take a closer look at the experience your organization or team provides. Put yourself into their shoes, and answer these questions from THEIR point of view. Use a scale of 1 to 5, with 5 being the highest.

How easy it is to do business with your organization/team?   Poor   Great
- On the phone 1 2 3 4 5
- Through the website 1 2 3 4 5
- In the office 1 2 3 4 5

How would you rate the friendliness of your organization/team? 1 2 3 4 5

How would you rate the knowledge of your organization/team? 1 2 3 4 5

How would you rate the quality of the product/service you receive? 1 2 3 4 5

How would you rate the value of the offering? 1 2 3 4 5

How would you rate the speed of delivery? 1 2 3 4 5

How would you rate the customer service and support you receive? 1 2 3 4 5

How accessible is the organization/team? 1 2 3 4 5

How would you rate the company's responsiveness to a complaint? 1 2 3 4 5

How satisfied are you with the action taken in response to a complaint? 1 2 3 4 5

How likely are you to seek out competitors to meet your needs? 1 2 3 4 5

How likely are you to continue working with this organization/team? 1 2 3 4 5

How disruptive would it be for the organization/team to have a change in leadership? 1 2 3 4 5

Five-Minute Customer Service Plan

If you are concerned that succession changes might result in the loss of customers, find ways now to strengthen those relationships and increase loyalty. The best way to uncover any problem areas? Ask! Use focus groups, polls, phone calls, or incentivized surveys to find out what your customers are thinking. Answer these questions to help identify potential opportunities for customer service improvements.

Our customers say they are "wowed" by every interaction with our organization.

_____ Yes! We're at the top of our game!

_____ Maybe. Depends on the day.

_____ Not so much.

Our customers think our service and follow-up are:

_____ Fabulous!

_____ Sometimes disappointing.

_____ Cringeworthy.

Where are the disconnects in your customer service today?

_____

_____

What could you do now to improve your customer experience?

In General _____

_____

During the Sales Process _____

_____

Through Service and Follow-Up _____

_____

What impact would those improvements have on your organization?

_____

_____

Five-Minute Vision Plan

Clarifying your organization's vision is an important part of your succession planning process. When you create a distinct and powerful vision, you can give everyone in the company a sense of purpose and a reason to strive for goals that are bigger than themselves. Answer these questions to help you fine tune your big-picture direction.

Distinguish between your company's mission and vision.

Your mission is what you do: *"We play baseball."*

Your vision is what you dream of accomplishing: *"We want to win the World Series."*

Mission: What does your organization actually do? Who do you serve?

_____

_____

_____

_____

_____

_____

_____

_____

_____

Vision: What does your organization dream of accomplishing long-term?

_____

_____

_____

_____

_____

_____

_____

_____

_____

_____

How will future changes in the following areas impact your organization's vision?

The Economy _____

_____

_____

_____

Financial Markets _____

_____

_____

_____

Technology _____

_____

_____

_____

Industry Regulations _____

_____

_____

_____

Competition _____

_____

_____

_____

Based on those anticipated changes, how might you adjust your vision to make it more compelling and keep it current over time? _____

_____

_____

_____

_____

_____

_____

_____

_____

Strategic Vision Planning Questions

As you work to clarify your organization's vision, gather input from your most important stakeholders. These include members of your current executive team, emerging leaders, and the Board of Directors. The questions below will guide your discussions as you brainstorm individually and as groups.

Think big.

- What are the big-picture benefits you deliver for your customers beyond your actual products/services (convenience, security, entertainment, comfort, etc.)?
- If your current products/services and delivery system become obsolete, how can you continue to provide the same benefits to your customers?
- How can you change the scope of your industry?
- What can you offer that your competition cannot?
- Do you have opportunities to meet other needs for your customers?
- Are there other target markets you can serve?
- How can you position your organization to be the recognized market leader?
- If you were going to start your company today, how would you do it differently?

Be proactive.

- What specific external factors have an impact on your business and industry—economic, financial, regulatory, technological, and competitive?
- What are the forecasts and projections for those external influences?
- How will those changes likely affect the products, services, and distribution methods you are currently using to serve your customers?
- What do you know about expected shifts in consumer preferences?
- How can you improve the way you build relationships with your customers in terms of communication, marketing, and sales?
- Can you provide solutions before your customers realize they have a problem?
- What steps can you take today to increase your efficiency, productivity, and performance in the years ahead?

- What can you do now to expand future revenue, profit, and shareholder value?

Stay flexible.
- How can you make adaptability one of your organization's core values?
- How can you use agility and innovation as a competitive advantage in the future?
- How can you respond to the changing needs of your customers at a lower opportunity cost than your competitors?

Succession Planning Models

Open Recruitment

This model involves the most comprehensive process, determining a specific succession path for every leadership position within the company.

Advantages:
- Increased employee engagement and morale
- Well trained and prepared candidates
- Transparent paths for advancement

Disadvantages:
- Ambitious scope could be overwhelming
- Significant commitment of time and resources
- Potential for talent gaps if candidates leave

Specialized Recruitment

This model limits succession planning to a more specialized group within the organization, including selected senior positions that are vital to the success of the business.

Advantages:
- Faster, easier process
- Reduced investment of resources

Disadvantages:
- Limited scope
- Excludes mid-level management

Outside Recruitment Model

This model guides companies to conduct a candidate search outside the organization or industry if the required talent isn't available in-house.

Advantages:

- Convenience of outsourcing to a recruiting firm
- An almost limitless talent pool
- Access to new leaders with fresh ideas

Disadvantages:

- Significant commitment of time and resources
- More in-depth training required for new hires
- Potential for less loyalty to the long-term vision

EXTERNAL CANDIDATES

CEO

VP   **VP**   VP   VP   **VP**

DIRECTORS, MANAGERS & SUPERVISORS

Succession Scheduling Tool

Succession Planning Task	Measurable Goal
Assemble planning team	
Partner with legal/tax advisors	
Clarify vision	
Assess bench strength	
Calculate turnover rates	
Identify critical roles for succession	
Determine retirement eligibility for key leaders	
Select planning model	
Choose org chart and reevaluate structure	
Develop skills criteria	
Design leader avatar	
Engage employees for feedback about careers	
Design talent pathways	
Create contingency plans	
Analyze HR inventory to determine outside needs	
Recruit and hire	
Streamline onboarding	
Train and develop	
Coach and mentor	
Improve engagement and accountability	
Upgrade rewards/incentives	
Communicate succession information	
Manage transitions	
Meet quarterly with team to monitor progress and update plan	

Start Date	Action Assigned	Team Member	DateComplete (or ongoing)

FOR THE PLANNING TEAM

Common Roles for Key Industries

These job descriptions may be helpful as you create the talent strategy for your succession plan. The first section includes common roles found in organizations today, while the second section provides a glimpse at new positions being incorporated into future-focused leadership teams.

CURRENT

1. **Chief Executive Officer (CEO):** the most senior executive in the corporation; responsible for all internal and external operations of the company.

2. **Chief Operations Officer (COO):** the executive responsible for all internal, day-to-day operations of the company.

3. **Chief Financial Officer (CFO):** the executive responsible for all of the company's financial affairs.

4. **Chief Sales Officer (CSO):** the executive responsible for the company's Sales leadership and Sales production.

5. **Chief Marketing Officer (CMO):** the executive responsible for all of the company's Marketing initiatives and programs (traditional and digital).

6. **Chief Technology Officer (CTO):** the executive responsible for the company's scientific and technology issues.

7. **Chief Information Officer (CIO):** the executive responsible for the Information Technology (IT) strategy and implementation.

8. **Chief Human Resources Officer (CHRO or Chief People Officer):** the executive responsible for all Human Resource management within the company.

9. **Chief Communications Officer (CCO):** the executive responsible for the company's internal and external communications and public relations.

10. **Chief Compliance Officer (CCO):** the executive responsible for the company's compliance with laws, regulatory requirements, policies, and procedures.

FUTURE

1. **Chief Ecosystem Officer (CECO):** the executive responsible for industry dynamics, partnership opportunities, and silo elimination.

2. **Chief User Experience Officer (CUEO):** the executive responsible for ensuring that in-store, online, and digital communications integrate for a seamless, positive user experience.

3. **Chief Automation Officer (CAO):** the executive responsible for identifying and integrating automation opportunities.

4. **Chief Freelance Relationship Officer (CFRO):** the executive responsible for managing and leading all freelance and contract employees.

5. **Chief Intellectual Property Officer (CIPO):** the executive responsible for all legal, compliance, and regulatory issues relating to the company's intellectual property.

6. **Chief Data Officer (CDO):** the executive responsible for streamlining, interpreting, and applying the data owned and gathered by the company.

7. **Chief Privacy Officer (CPO):** the executive responsible for ensuring data privacy, fending off potential data breaches, and handling the public response to any security lapses.

| 143

Five-Minute Skills Assessment

The primary purpose of succession planning is to be ready with replacement talent when someone in a key position leaves the company. The only way to be prepared for that is to fully understand the knowledge, skills, and experience required for success in that role. By completing the assessment below for each of your succession-targeted positions, you'll have a head start on clarifying the exact job criteria to help identify the most qualified candidates.

Title _____

Projected Employee Departure Date _____

Job description _____

_____

_____

How has this position evolved over time? _____

_____

_____

What challenges will the next leader likely face? *(i.e., new regulations, foreign competition, evolving customer preferences, changing technology, mergers and acquisitions, etc.)* _____

_____

_____

What functional competencies will the successor need? _____

_____

_____

What leadership skills will be required for the successor? _____

_____

_____

What are the top three attributes for the person in this position?

1. _____
_____

2. _____
_____

3. _____
_____

How will this job change in the next 3-5 years? _____
_____
_____
_____

If the previous job description is no longer accurate, how would you update it?
_____
_____
_____

What other relevant factors need to be considered?
_____
_____
_____
_____
_____
_____
_____
_____
_____
_____
_____
_____

FOR THE PLANNING TEAM

Leadership Competency Assessment

If you can more narrowly define the qualifications for each targeted position on your organization chart, you increase your odds of finding successors who are a perfect match and enable seamless transitions. Prioritizing leadership competencies is a great way to do that. For each job in question, list the top five leadership competencies required for success. We've included some options.

Job Title _____

Top Leadership Competencies for Success in this Position

1. _____
2. _____
3. _____
4. _____
5. _____

Business Judgment: the ability to make solid, sound decisions in the best interests of the organization's long-term health.

Conflict Management: the ability to immediately identify tension, address conflict, and help others work toward acceptable solutions.

Crisis Management: the ability to quickly analyze, grasp, and navigate challenging situations.

Decision-Making: a proven track record of analyzing options and making smart choices.

Emotional Intelligence: the ability to easily understand and connect with other people, even adjusting communication styles to better relate to them.

Entrepreneurship: the ability to take calculated risks in pursuing a unique business idea.

Financial Acumen: a strong understanding and expertise in financial matters, both internal and external.

Industry Knowledge: a solid grasp of the history, current challenges, and future opportunities within the industry.

Influence: the ability to inspire others in the areas of self-organization, collaboration, and shared commitment to achieving goals.

Interpersonal Skills: the ability to communicate and interact with others in a way that generates respect and trust.

Moral Courage: the confidence to do the right thing for your people, your organization, and your customers.

Strategic Thinking: the ability to carefully think through challenges and opportunities before developing and implementing a strategy.

Talent Development: the ability to attract, develop, and retain top talent.

Vision: the ability to craft, communicate, and engage others in the long-term direction and goals of the organization.

Leadership Avatar Exercise

By definition, an avatar is an icon or representation of something else. For the purposes of succession planning, you can use this concept of creating an avatar to help define the essence of the perfect successor for your top executive. In other words, you can identify the ideal attributes, characteristics, skills, and talents of the best possible person to assume control of the company when your current leader departs. This succession avatar will give you a more quantitative way to evaluate candidates as you compare them with the fictitious gold standard.

1.　Select an elite team to help build your succession planning avatar. Limit the group to no more than five, and choose colleagues and peers who can add strategic and practical perspectives. Team members include:

_____

_____

_____

_____

_____

2.　Make a list of your most outstanding employees, including those you would not want to lose (especially to competitors).

_____

_____

_____

_____

_____

3.　Write down all of the skills and talents exhibited by these top-level employees that make them successful within your organization and your industry.

_____

_____

_____

_____

_____

FOR SUCCESSION-TARGETED EMPLOYEES

4. Supplement that list with any other skills, talents, attributes, and competencies that would be required for the ideal version of your top executive.

   _____

   _____

   _____

   _____

   _____

5. Bring your succession avatar to life by using those lists to vividly describe your perfect incoming leader using specific, detailed terms. *"Our next leader is...*

   _____

   _____

   _____

   _____

   _____

6. Visualize the human reflection of that description, and use the avatar as the benchmark for your talent search. While some people discount this exercise, it is extremely powerful and can tangibly elevate the quality of your chosen successor.

   _____

   _____

   _____

   _____

   _____

Five-Minute Career Plan

Sometimes we get so busy with the daily challenges of work that we neglect to look at the big picture of our careers, as well as those of the people on our teams. Take a moment to complete the statements below, based on your workday and the tasks you do for your job. Are you engaged in positive, productive, and fulfilling activities? If not, think about how you can change that by shifting your career path.

Passion
I get excited when I talk about:

_____

Energy
I feel energized when I get to work on:

_____

Focus
My perfect workday is when I complete:

_____

Satisfaction
The best part of my week happens when:

_____

Opportunities
I can move my career forward in this job by:
doing more _____,
interacting with _____,
and asking _____ for help.

Fulfillment
I can help other people with their careers or businesses by:

_____

_____

_____

Five-Minute Recruiting Plan

Attracting, engaging, and hiring great talent can be a challenge in today's complex marketplace. One way to improve your recruiting is to borrow a few lessons from the sports world! Below, we've provided you with five strategies used by sports recruiters. Translate those into the business environment by answering the questions that follow.

1. **Sports recruiters go where the talent is.**
    Where can you find your future talent? Where do they work/live?

    _____

2. **Sports recruiters look for potential.**
    What does great potential look like in your job candidates? How can you screen for that?

    _____

3. **Sports recruiters plan years in advance for depth on the bench.**
    What talents, skills, and abilities will the organization need in the next year? In 3 years? In 5 years?

    _____

    Where do you have depth now? What's lacking? Are you developing employees to improve that bench strength?

    _____

4. **Sports recruiters have contingency plans, knowing players can be hurt, transferred, or not work out as well as they hoped.**
    Do you have a plan to replace people if they leave?

    _____

    What positions in your organization are the most critical?

    _____

5. **Sports recruiters are constantly scouting for talent.**
    Do you have an ongoing plan to identify and attract great talent?

    _____

    _____

Leadership Development Plan Assessment

Please answer the following questions to help us understand your career goals and ultimately design a customized development plan for your long-term success with the organization.

Name _____

Current Title _____

_____

_____

_____

What part of your current job do you absolutely love? _____

_____

_____

What part of your current job is your least favorite? _____

_____

_____

_____

What would you like to be doing more of? _____

_____

_____

_____

Are we challenging you enough? Why or why not? _____

_____

_____

_____

What role would you like to play within this organization long-term? _____

_____

_____

_____

FOR SUCCESSION-TARGETED EMPLOYEES

What role do your see yourself playing in 3-5 years? _____

_____

_____

_____

What role do you view as a short-term goal? _____

_____

_____

_____

On a scale of 1 to 5, how ready are you to take on the next level of responsibility?

1 *(Not at all)*   **2**   **3**   **4**   **5** *(Ready now)*

What skills do you have now that align with your desired career path? _____

_____

_____

_____

What skills do you want to develop to prepare for advancement? _____

_____

_____

_____

What is your personal plan of action to ensure that you are ready to move up?

_____

_____

_____

What support do you need from the organization to help you become ready?

_____

_____

_____

If you were in charge, what would you change about the organization?

_____

_____

_____

30-60-90 Onboarding Guide

To create an optimal onboarding process for new employees, use this guide to define expectations for the first 30, 60, and 90 days with the company. This includes parameters for what you expect from them and what they can expect from you. When you share ownership of onboarding with employees, you accelerate the development process and increase the positive impact.

In the first 30 days,
employees should expect to gain a strong overview of the organization:

- Receive a set of milestone goals to achieve within the onboarding process.
- Receive an overview of their job descriptions.
- Learn the organization's history, vision, mission, and values.
- Take a full tour of the facility or facilities.
- Explore the company website and understand its features/components.
- Be introduced to the corporate culture.
- Learn the key positions and players within the organization.
- Shadow other leaders and departments to better understand the general operation of the company and its revenue-producing processes.
- Participate in at least two (2) one-on-one meetings with their managers to discuss job requirements, ideas, and expectations.

In the first 60 days,
employees should expect to gain clarity about their roles and contributions:

- Complete everything on the 30-day checklist.
- Identify a detailed list of tasks associated with their current roles.
- Participate in learning opportunities for skill development (i.e., computer system, HR forms, sales process, etc.).
- Request any additional training needed beyond the core programs offered (i.e., technical applications, coaching and mentoring, etc.).
- Attend team meetings and interact with peers.
- Learn to engage with customers, even if that's not part of their roles.
- Understand how their departments work and how their team deliverables help to meet corporate goals.

- Work with Human Resources to learn the review process and become familiar with how their success will be measured.
- Meet with their managers to review their progress and request feedback at the end of 60 days.

In the first 90 days,

employees should expect to play an active role in achieving team objectives:

- Complete everything on the 60-day checklist.
- Fill in any knowledge gaps and complete training programs.
- Meet job requirements and fulfill the duties of their roles.
- Actively participate in team meetings and coaching sessions.
- Strengthen relationships and connections with other team members.
- Collaborate effectively, providing feedback and input to others.
- Participate in developing solutions for team challenges.
- Make significant progress toward goals and key performance indicators.
- Prepare for final onboarding session with their managers, developing reviews of their own performance, ideas for next steps, and strategies for continued growth.

FOR CURRENT LEADERS

Leadership Improvement Plan

The most effective leaders are constantly seeking to improve themselves, but that requires commitment, focus, and effort. If you've inadvertently become complacent, answer the questions below to jumpstart your improvement plan.

1. **What can you improve to become a better leader for your teams?**

    _____

    _____

    _____

2. **How can you become an even better supervisor for your direct reports?**

    _____

    _____

    _____

3. **What can you improve to become a better peer?** *(i.e., helping coworkers be more successful at their jobs or being more supportive of your boss)*

    _____

    _____

    _____

4. **Based on the answers above, pick three areas you are committed to improving right away.**

    - Branding
    - Budgeting
    - Coaching
    - Collaboration
    - Communication
    - Conflict Resolution
    - Creativity
    - Customer Contact
    - Delegation
    - Email Management
    - Expectation Management
    - Flexibility
    - Listening
    - Motivation
    - Negotiating
    - Policy Enforcement
    - Positivity
    - Providing Feedback
    - Relationship Building
    - Sales/Marketing
    - Scheduling
    - Strategic Planning
    - Teambuilding
    - Other _____

5. How can you take action to make these improvements?

- Articles
- Books
- Conferences
- Google
- Mastermind Group
- Mentor Guidance
- Networking
- Philanthropy/Service

- Role Playing
- Team Discussions
- Training Courses
- Videos
- Webinars
- YouTube
- Other _____

6. Use the space below to write out your specific plan for leadership improvement, including the time frame for achieving your goals.

_____

_____

_____

_____

_____

_____

_____

_____

_____

_____

_____

_____

_____

_____

_____

Five-Minute Employee Engagement Plan

When employee engagement is low, organizations suffer. Leaders can make a significant improvement in engagement by having the right conversations with their direct reports. We've provided some talking point starters and questions below with room for you to complete the thoughts about a particular employee. You can use this page as a reference during one-on-one interactions.

Communicate how employees are connected to the corporate vision.

The vision for our organization is: _____

_____

You are helping us achieve that because you provide: _____

_____

We rely on you for: _____

_____

Keep employees challenged.

What particular skills and strengths do you want to utilize more? _____

_____

Are there specific projects you want to be more involved in? _____

_____

Do you want more responsibility? If so, in what way? _____

_____

Focus on development.

What training would be helpful for you? _____

_____

What would you like to learn next? _____

_____

Are you interested in receiving coaching or being connected with a mentor?

_____

How can we help you reach your full potential? _____

_____

Improve the environment.

What do you like best about your work space? _____

_____

What would make work more enjoyable for you? _____

_____

Are there any tools or resources that would help you be more efficient and successful? _____

_____

Provide positive feedback.

I have noticed you are really great at: _____

_____

You did an excellent job of handling: _____

_____

I'm always impressed by your ability to: _____

_____

FOR THE PLANNING TEAM

Succession Accountability Tracker

These questions can be used as a guide for discussions in quarterly meetings with your succession planning team. Addressing each of these issues will help to keep your team accountable and maximize the efficiency of your time together.

1. **What are the top three accomplishments you have made with your succession plan?**

    _____

    _____

    _____

2. **Have you identified all of the critical roles for your plan?**

    _____

    _____

    _____

3. **What percentage of those critical roles currently have a successor?**

    _____

    _____

    _____

4. **What actions can you take today to start identifying successors for the other critical roles?**

    _____

    _____

    _____

5. **What communication have you had with successor candidates? Is more needed?**

    _____

    _____

    _____

6. **What training and development is under way for successor candidates?**

    _____

    _____

    _____

FOR THE PLANNING TEAM

7. What are the top three challenges you are facing with the plan right now?

   _____

   _____

   _____

8. What updates do you need to make to the plan? Are there any gaps? Is it time to expand the scope?

   _____

   _____

   _____

9. What are the next three positions to fill or actions to take?

   _____

   _____

   _____

10. Who is responsible for the next steps?

    _____

    _____

    _____

11. What are the deadlines?

    _____

    _____

    _____

12. What is the date and time of your next meeting?

    _____

    _____

    _____

Change Management for Leaders

Most people struggle with change. That means leaders have an opportunity to help their teams work through things like personnel changes and reorganizations by carefully managing and communicating the process. Follow the steps below and answer the questions to give more structure to your change management techniques.

1. **Recognize the emotional red flags.**
    What signs have you noticed that could indicate your team members are struggling with change? *(For example: fear, frustration, uncertainty, stress, etc.)*

    _____

    _____

    _____

2. **Keep your team members informed.**
    What information can you share about the changes?

    _____

    _____

    _____

    What's the best format, word choice, tone, and timing to deliver that communication?

    _____

    _____

    _____

3. **Listen to concerns.**
    How can you improve your active listening skills? _____

    _____

    _____

4. **What open-ended questions could lead the conversation?** *(For example: How will this change impact you personally? What worries you the most?)*

    _____

    _____

    _____

5. **Remain calm and reassuring.**
    How can you communicate those qualities, verbally and nonverbally?

    _____

    _____

    _____

6. **Be honest about the future.**
    Managing change doesn't mean sugar-coating difficult realities. Do you
    have team members who need to know the truth about their opportunities for
    advancement or about the skill deficits that are holding them back?

    _____

    _____

    _____

7. **Demonstrate trust.**
    What projects and responsibilities could you share with your team members to
    develop their confidence in coping with change?

    _____

    _____

    _____

Course Correction Plan

Succession planning is a process that involves continuous changes. To keep your plan on track, closely monitor your results and be ready to make course corrections as needed.

1. What is working well with your succession plan? How can you continue that success?

    _____

    _____

    _____

2. What is causing frustration and uncertainty? How can you mitigate those issues?

    _____

    _____

    _____

3. What assumptions are you making in the planning process? Are you missing anything? Are there some assumptions you should avoid?

    _____

    _____

    _____

4. How can you improve your process?

    _____

    _____

    _____

5. How can you improve your results?

    _____

    _____

    _____

Obstacles Assessment

Choosing a successor for a family business can be an uncomfortable task, but it's also a critically urgent one. If you own a family business and recognize you've been avoiding this subject, answer the questions below to help you identify the specific obstacles that are holding you back.

1. **I don't know of anyone who is as committed to the business as I am.**
    ☐ Yes   ☐ No   ☐ Maybe

2. **I keep hoping a family member will want to step up and take over.**
    ☐ Yes   ☐ No   ☐ Maybe

3. **I'm worried that a family member will want to step up and take over.**
    ☐ Yes   ☐ No   ☐ Maybe

4. **I don't want to stir up family drama.**
    ☐ Yes   ☐ No   ☐ Maybe

5. **I'm concerned that someone will ruin the company, along with my legacy.**
    ☐ Yes   ☐ No   ☐ Maybe

6. **I'm worried about showing favoritism to a particular family member.**
    ☐ Yes   ☐ No   ☐ Maybe

7. **I don't think I could trust an outsider to run the family business.**
    ☐ Yes   ☐ No   ☐ Maybe

8. **I'm concerned that a non-family member wouldn't be fully engaged.**
    ☐ Yes   ☐ No   ☐ Maybe

9. **I don't want to make a mistake.**
    ☐ Yes   ☐ No   ☐ Maybe

10. **I've got plenty of time before I have to worry about succession.**
    ☐ Yes   ☐ No   ☐ Maybe

RESOURCE GUIDE

Be Amazing or Go Home: Seven Customer Service Habits that Create Confidence with Everyone
Book by Shep Hyken
www.amazon.com

Handing Over the Reigns: A Concise Guide to Succession Planning
Book by Richard J. Bryan
www.amazon.com

How to Make Your Family Business Last
Book by Mitzi Perdue
www.amazon.com

In Case of Emergency, Break Glass!
Book by Mary Kelly
www.amazon.com

The Leadership Mindset: How Today's Successful Business Leaders Think
Book by Joe Calloway
www.amazon.com

Organization Chart Templates
Helpful Links to Template Options
www.WhoComesNext.com

Own It: Redefining Responsibility
Book by Meridith Elliott Powell
www.amazon.com

The Successful Family Business: A Proactive Plan for Managing The Family and The Business
Book by Edward Hess
www.amazon.com

"Three Strategies to Get Your Succession Plan Moving"
Article by Meridith Elliott Powell
https://meridithelliottpowell.com/new-role-succession-planning/

"The Time to Start Succession Planning is NOW!"
Article by Mary Kelly
https://productiveleaders.com/succession-planning/

WhoComesNext.com
Dedicated Book Website

- *Online Course: Who Comes Next? Leadership Succession Planning Made Easy*
- *Free Webinar*
- *Book Bonuses*
- *Free Succession Articles*

Why Leaders Fail and the Seven Prescriptions for Success
Book by Mary Kelly and Peter Stark
www.amazon.com

ABOUT THE AUTHORS

Mary C. Kelly | Ph.D., Commander, U.S. Navy (ret)
CEO, Productive Leaders

Mary specializes in leadership growth that helps organizations improve their profitability and productivity, especially in finance, insurance, real estate, and manufacturing. One of the first female graduates of the Naval Academy, Mary served 25 years on active duty, mostly in Asia, leading multi-cultural teams in nine countries. Her remarkable career of service included working as an intelligence officer, a chief of police, an HR director, and a chief of staff, as well as training more than 40,000 military personnel.

Mary has been a leadership and economics professor at the Naval Academy, the Air Force Academy, and Hawaii Pacific University. She has written 13 business books, including her best-seller, *Master Your World* (named a "must read" by MENSA and MOAA), and her latest award-winner, *Why Leaders Fail and the 7 Prescriptions for Success* (profiled in *Forbes* and *Success* magazines).

Today, Mary is a popular conference keynote speaker and leadership adviser working with businesses, associations, and government agencies. She offers programs that are content rich, highly entertaining, and strategically designed to help her clients get results.

mary@productiveleaders.com | www.ProductiveLeaders.com

Meridith Elliott Powell | M.B.A.
Business Growth, Sales and Leadership Expert

Meridith is a business strategist, keynote speaker, and award-winning author with expertise in business growth, sales, and leadership strategies. She has been named **One of the Top 15 Business Growth Experts to Watch** by *Currency Fair* and **One of the Top 20 Sales Experts To Follow** by LinkedIn.

A former C-suite executive, Meridith has extensive experience in the banking, healthcare, and finance industries. She has earned a number of prestigious accreditations including Master Certified Strategist, Executive Coach and Certified Speaking Professional (a designation held by less than 12% of professional speakers), and Master Certified DISC Trainer and Coach (facilitating and coaching thousands in that program).

Meridith shares her business expertise with organizations through cutting-edge messages rooted in real-life examples and real-world knowledge. She is the author of five books, including *Winning In The Trust & Value Economy* (USA Best Book Awards finalist) and *Own It: Redefining Responsibility – Stories of Power, Freedom & Purpose*. Her latest book, *The Best Sales Book Ever!*, is positioned to be the next best-seller for high-performing salespeople and their leaders. It also received the coveted Gold Award from the Nonfiction Authors Association.

mere@valuespeaker.com | www.MeridithElliottPowell.com

CONTACT US

www.WhoComesNext.com

Please visit our site for additional content and frequent updates.

Mary C. Kelly
www.ProductiveLeaders.com

mary@productiveleaders.com
Office: (719) 357-7360
Mobile: (443) 995-8663

Follow Mary:

Meridith Elliott Powell
www.MeridithElliottPowell.com

mere@valuespeaker.com
Office: (888) 526-9998
Mobile: (828) 243-3510

Follow Meridith: